THE **PERFECT EDUCATION** FOR YOUR LEARNER

A SUCCESSFUL EDUCATION

How to tailor an education to perfectly
fit your unique child's needs.

Is your child struggling to engage in learning?
It's not your child.
It's the method.

MARTA **OBIOLS LLISTAR**

ARGYLE FOX
PUBLISHING

TABLE OF CONTENTS

To my readers, who asked how to unschool
and demanded a second book.

FOREWORD

ON MY BEDROOM WALL HANGS THE Declaration of Independence. I found it in one of my dad's junk boxes when we were in the midst of unpacking boxes from the move. My parents sold the house years ago, I believe I was thirteen, to move to a cheaper house so they could homeschool us with better funds. When I saw that old brown document written by the founding fathers, I wanted it right away. I wanted it hanging on my wall, and my mom offered to frame it. That's my mom, always trying to provide for our needs.

The Declaration of Independence is an important symbol because it's a reminder of what Americans should strive for every day. It says life and liberty and the pursuit of happiness. Which is exactly how my mother has raised us.

When I found out I was not going back to school, I was relieved. There, I felt like an outcast. I remember not having any friends.

Once we started the new life without school, I felt free. I enjoyed countless hours and days playing with my brother and sister. We enjoyed life.

Not going to school was such a positive experience

for me growing up. We joined a group of homeschoolers who met once a week at a park. The group consisted of about thirty kids or more of all ages, races, and religious beliefs. It was there that I met my best friends. I love my friends. They inspire me and motivate me to be a better person every day.

All my friends are homeschool kids. Not unschooled, but homeschooled. In every activity I've participated in that wasn't homeschool-related, like archery and my job at the coffee shop, there has always been another homeschool person, making the situation less awkward and accepting. However, since my brother started playing soccer two years ago, he has always been the only homeschooler, and it seems like his teammates have never heard of homeschooling. He always has to explain and answer all the typical questions. People are interesting. They don't understand we can learn and have friends without school.

Even though my parents and I have different political views and interests, they have always supported my interests, making me feel uplifted and respected. Unschooling has given me the freedom to follow my passion and live a life that excites me every day.

I learned everything I wanted to learn from the comfort of my home by reading books, using my computer, my friends' parents' classes, and from other classes I chose to take. I learned, and I had plenty of free time to do other things that I enjoyed. I played a lot in the street with my neighbors and at the park and woods with my friends.

The internet is a great tool for learning. Documentaries, blogs, articles, and podcasts—I used all of them to educate myself. The experts in one specific field are not in the school classroom. No, they are out in the world. They have written books and made documentaries and podcasts. Those experts teach us. There is no need to be in the classroom waiting for a teacher to feed us knowledge. I learned astrophysics by reading Neil deGrasse Tyson's *Astrophysics For People in a Hurry*.

Right now my life is pretty busy. I'm a part-time barista, a coach for a semi-professional eSports team, and a writer. My main focus is to get my science fiction novel published. I'm hoping that with my novel I can inspire aspiring science fiction writers with my stories.

I hope one day children from countries where home education is illegal will be allowed to grow up the same way I did.

Perhaps now, with the famous singer Alanis Morissette and entrepreneur Elon Musk openly discussing unschooling their children, and considering the experiences of scientist Erik Demaine and singer-songwriter Billie Eilish, who grew up unschooled, people will start listening. There are other ways of learning besides going to school.

Self-directed learning worked for me.

Jaume Obiols Gorman
Author of the upcoming book *Ghost in the Void*

A
SUCCESSFUL
EDUCATION

What children need is not new and better curricula but access to more and more of the real world; plenty of time and space to think over their experiences, and to use fantasy and play to make meaning out of them; and advice, road maps, guidebooks, to make it easier for them to get where they want to go (not where we think they ought to go), and to find out what they want to find out.

—John Holt

INTRODUCTION

ARE YOU TIRED OF THE ENDLESS SEARCH FOR the perfect school or education for your child, only to be disappointed time and again?

As a parent and a teacher who has experienced the same frustration, looking for the perfect place for my kids to learn and for me to work, I know all too well the feeling of hopelessness that can accompany the pursuit of the ideal program. But here's the stark truth: that program simply does not exist. No matter how hard you try, you won't find it. There is no one-size-fits-all solution that can meet the needs of every child, but you can create it. You, dear reader, are in charge of creating the perfect program for your child, one that's tailor-made for their unique needs and strengths.

This book aims to help you give your children a successful education. I have educated my three children successfully and want to help you do the same.

My elder son, twenty years old, has become a writer. His first novel will be published soon. He has started writing his second novel. His education led him to accomplish his goal. He is an author.

My daughter is now seventeen and getting ready to

audition for a college in Europe. She is a phenomenal aerialist athlete and wants to specialize in corde lisse (climbing a rope and doing acrobatic tricks in the air). If admitted, she will receive a circus arts degree and a contract with a circus company. She wants to be part of a circus family and perform aerial moves on a rope. This college will give her the tools to succeed.

My youngest, educated freely without school until age fourteen, is attending his first year of high school in a public school. His passion for playing soccer led him there. Here in the U.S., sports are often associated with high schools. Although many soccer clubs hold practices after school, all players typically leave their club to play for their high school team during soccer season. My son and his personal experience show that high school soccer offers him better training opportunities. To him, success is becoming a soccer player or any job that doesn't tie you to an office nine to five. He learned and started to invest and has *rich businessman* written all over his DNA. I know he'll be successful.

And I am successful too. I found the best way to educate my kids and to enjoy being an educator. I have raised three independent individuals who were free to become whoever they wanted to be. By "free," I mean I did not impose my own decisions on them. Instead, I tried to erase the mentality I grew up with: "You have to go to college or you won't get a good-paying job."

I tried to show my children that people in non-academic careers can also be successful. I needed to avoid perpetuating the stigma that only people with specific jobs can be successful while others cannot.

Success is relative since everyone has a different definition of it. Some people believe that success is synonymous with happiness, while others associate it with accumulating wealth. Some consider achieving the highest academic success, such as obtaining a Ph.D., to be successful. Most parents worry about their children's future, wanting them to have a safe and successful life. They often convince their children to attend college to secure a good job. However, have you ever asked your children what they consider a good job? Is college what they truly desire?

How my parents and other parents view success differs significantly from mine, which has taught me a valuable lesson. As a parent, do you want to boast to your friends and family about the successful children you have created or would you rather understand what success means to your children and help them achieve it?

Let's help our children be successful. Whether this means attending IB prestigious school or not, attending college or technical school, getting a blue-collar job, or becoming an entrepreneur. Are you ready to let go of what success means to you and listen to what success means to your kids?

Are you ready to educate your children successfully?

We can best help children learn, not by deciding what we think they should learn and thinking of ingenious ways to teach it to them, but by making the world, as far as we can, accessible to them, paying serious attention to what they do, answering their questions—if they have any—and helping them explore the things they are most interested in.

—John Holt

WHAT'S A SUCCESSFUL EDUCATION?

A SUCCESSFUL EDUCATION PUTS STUDENTS IN control of their learning, and it starts with empowerment rather than compliance.

A successful education starts with paying attention to the learners' needs and providing for those needs. It doesn't start with what society and culture think students need; it doesn't start by listening to chatter that goes against your instinct, gut, and heart.

Our society has lost its common sense. Young children require the care and presence of their mother or primary caretaker. We cannot delegate the responsibility of educating our children when they are vulnerable and in their early years. So why does society keep pushing us to send our children to daycares and schools? Children naturally desire to be with their mothers. As they grow older and become more independent, they detach from their primary caretakers and enjoy attending activities without them. If your children do not enjoy daycare, preschool, or the nanny, they may still need to be with you and are not yet ready to move on. Your children can still have a successful education without attending an IB preschool. By staying home with you rather than attending preschool, your child may have a greater chance of success.

A successful education is an organic and natural process that allows children to become who they are destined to be by studying, learning, and pursuing their interests. Success is defined by the individual and should not be imposed upon them by others.

Education will only be successful when we allow children to learn at their own pace, respecting their learning rhythm and curiosity. This means letting them spend days, weeks, and even months pursuing specific interests, free from coerced education. Successful education is the type that allows children to be who they are without judgment. Most importantly, success is when children never lose their hunger for learning. Successful education involves adults helping and supporting students to achieve their goals and dreams while also allowing them to determine if those dreams are realistic. It respects their interpretation of what a successful life looks like.

Educating this way is known as self-directed education by clinical, research, and educational psychologists. Some of us call it "unschooling" because we don't want to replicate the school system at home. We try to forget the school rhythm, patterns, grades, and standards to avoid being influenced by them and really see our children and let them lead their learning. It is a form of learning where the child is involved in their education. It is targeted, unique to the child, and the most natural and joyful state of education. It creates a happy childhood and adolescence, leading to a happy, satisfying, and productive adulthood. Yes, it can also lead to higher education if the person wishes, and they can still succeed and get "good" jobs.

How to provide a successful education

The best education is one that satisfies the student. Start by respecting your children's interests, curiosity, natural rhythm, and preferred learning methods. Sometimes, what is best for your child may not align with the choices made by the majority of families. Don't compare yourself with them. To truly educate your children, you must empower them to become who they want to be.

Don't control what children have to learn; trust that they will know what they need. Do they need reading skills, writing skills, or counting skills? They will eagerly learn them.

Let's look at a successful education when parents and teachers respect the child's natural rhythm. Let me show you the truth about learning.

They play.

Children will play for years, and if you provide them with a rich environment and take them to different places, they will learn tremendously while playing and living their daily lives.

As they grow older, their play becomes more sophisticated. There's no difference between playtime and learning time when learning self-directed. They are in a state of constant inquiry, trying new experiences and following their interests.

Around teenagerhood, kids often go through a phase when they seem hungry for knowledge and skills. They dive deep into them and start to plan their path.

To ensure a successful education, you must provide a friendly environment for everyone. An atmosphere of trust, comfort, and support, where children and adolescents can explore, play, and learn (these three words are the same) with pleasure, where they feel comfortable, they trust you, and they can ask for help if needed.

Several key factors are linked to the effectiveness of the learning process. Our emotional response to a learning experience is crucial in determining future motivation and self-esteem around an area of learning. By acknowledging and building on children's interests, we help children feel valued as individuals who are experts in their own life experiences.

How meaningful a learning experience is perceived to be is also crucial. We tend to be more engaged when we see learning as valuable to ourselves and our lives. It's vital to observe and interact with your children so you can provide a meaningful learning experience.

A successful education system should prioritize psychological comfort. Creating a space where children can experience no pressure or stress and feel free to be themselves is essential. Homework and exams should only be given if they are enjoyable for the children and wanted by them.

I was privileged to observe how my children's natural

curiosity helped them learn. Now it's my responsibility to show you how to do the same. I educated my kids, and so can you. You can give them a successful education too. Well, I didn't exactly do it. I facilitated and provided what they needed, which made it successful.

Are you ready to give your students total control over what and how they learn, their educational environment, and how they are evaluated? Studies have shown that when people determine what to learn, they retain the subject significantly better than if someone else decides what they should know.

"But all they do is play?" a lot of you may ask, shocked and doubtful of the effectiveness of such an education.

Yes! Playing is learning, exploring, practicing, and experiencing. Play is the ultimate learning modality, and children have an innate desire to play constantly, from the moment they open their eyes in the morning until the moment they finally close them in exhaustion at night.

Children rapidly acquire vast amounts of knowledge and skills through various types of play. They construct causal maps and world models, develop counterfactual reasoning and theory of mind, and cultivate multiple physical, intellectual, and emotional attributes and skills. Different types of play, such as symbolic, rough-and-tumble, or locomotor play, offer specific learning opportunities. And all of this happens naturally as children follow their instincts, pursue their passions, and simply enjoy their lives.

There is so much learning that occurs just by living

your life. Our brains are much better at learning from experiences than gathering information from concepts. Experiences are much more effective in aiding learning.

What is most important and valuable about the home as a base for children's growth into the world is not that it is a better school than the schools, but that it isn't a school at all.

—John Holt

THE ORIGINAL NEVER FADES

YOU ARE EAGER TO FIND OUT WHAT A successful education is. First, you must learn about self-directed education, called child-led learning or unschooling—the original way of learning.

This type of education is achievable through alternative approaches such as homeschooling, democratic schools, or free schools, prioritizing self-directed learning and allowing children to take charge of their education. Alternatively, traditional schools can support this type of education if children attend willingly and by choice rather than being forced. Learning without attending school is not new or radical; humans have successfully educated their young ones without school for centuries. Our current school system is a new experiment. Sending children to school to be segregated by age, separated from the community, and learning the same exact curriculum is a radical idea with counterproductive results.

That said, I'm not against public education. I think it's wonderful that a free resource to educate children exists and is available to everyone. I am opposed to how they teach and treat children. When you impose education, children either don't want to learn or want to learn to impress the adults. When you show, offer, and make education easy to reach without boundaries, children not only want to learn, they soak in it and thrive.

Nobody likes to learn unnecessary knowledge, especially if it doesn't interest them. However, we all have an innate desire to learn. It's time to stop teaching kids and allow them to learn. A child-led education that doesn't impose what and when to learn is the education that enables children to learn naturally because they want to learn and enjoy doing so.

You ensure success by allowing your kids to choose what and when to learn. You won't have to spend time motivating them because you allow their inherent motivation to take its course. When a school or homeschool curriculum is designed for everyone, it neglects those who fall outside the average. Our kids are unique, and their education should be tailored to fit them. We must provide the resources and experts our children need.

There are two different Latin roots of the English word "education." "Educare" means to train or mold, while "educere" means to lead out. To succeed in our kids' education, we need to focus on *educere*, to lead out, instead of *educare*, because molding our kids can be harmful. As Jess Lair famously said, "Children are not things to be molded, but are people to be unfolded."

So many families have successfully educated their children outside the school system. This type of education has restored their joy.

Kids feel rejected when a school, teacher, or educational plan doesn't match their learning style. They can't learn in an environment that keeps failing them.

Home education provides freedom and a wealth of benefits for the entire family. The ability to customize education, create a healthy social environment, achieve better academic results, and strengthen family relationships are why many families are turning to non-traditional schooling. It is a superior alternative in all respects.

It's time for a change. The fact that schools exist doesn't mean you should send your child to them without paying attention to their preferences. Some children like to attend school, while others don't. Ask them if they want to learn at home or go to school, and don't be afraid of their answer. How they learn should be their choice, which might change over time.

Are you fearful of educating your child outside of the traditional norm? It may seem daunting initially, but it's simply a new experience. The more you do it, the less intimidating it becomes. To help ease your fears, arm yourself with knowledge about alternative forms of education and connect with other families experienced in this lifestyle. By meeting others and learning about this type of life, you can dispel any doubts or worries. Many resources—including books, articles, podcasts, blogs, courses, and coaches—can provide you with all the necessary information. Thank you for choosing this book as one of your resources.

Some of you already know the advantages of home education. You are tremendously interested in learning how to facilitate it in a way that works well for your child. Some of you want to embrace your kids' self-directed learning because you understand how to educate successfully but don't know how to start.

Here's how. Let's look at how to give our children sole responsibility for their education, learning methods, evaluation, and environment.

The original never fades. Home education is the new black.

*P*eople should be free to find or make for themselves the kinds of educational experience they want their children to have.

—John Holt

LAW

FIRST THINGS FIRST: AS MUCH AS I WOULD LIKE
for all of us to be free to do whatever we want and tailor
our children's education accordingly, we must abide by
rules and laws. In the United States, we are free to choose
any education we want for our children, but in other
countries, the government mandates how its citizens
should be educated. If you and your children cannot find
a school that suits your needs, and you choose to educate
at home to tailor the perfect education for your children
to achieve success, you must be aware of the rules set by
your government.

Every country and every state in the U.S. has different laws regarding the education of children who do not
attend school. To avoid getting in trouble, it is crucial
to research, study, and inform yourself about the laws
and regulations in your area and follow them accordingly. For example, in Chile, I've been told by a Chilean
homeschool mom that families are not required to report
to the government, but in the U.S., it depends on the
state. Only sick children, athletes, musicians, and actors
can receive education outside traditional schools in some
countries.

In contrast, in certain countries, it is illegal for families to educate their children outside the formal school system.

An easy way to find the rules of your state or country is to search online. Write the name of your state or country and the word "homeschool" on your search engine, or write "homeschool laws" followed by the name of your state or country. Usually, the Department of Education website in your state or country will appear with information on home study and the necessary documents and procedures to follow.

Additionally, other websites provide valuable information from other families who have already gone through the process.

If you are not interested in education without school and want a successful education for your child, search online for schools that practice conscious education and self-directed education. Those schools are called democratic schools, free schools, and self-directed education centers. You should search for Sudbury Valley and Summerhill online to learn more about these schools.

If it is illegal in your country to educate your child at home, you can read a letter from my friend at the end of this book. She left the Netherlands to provide education for her children outside of the school system. Some families may leave their country to do what they believe is best for their children. However, if leaving the country is not an option for you, I am deeply sorry and wish I knew how to offer assistance.

Online resources I recommend include:
- hslda.org
- sudburyvalley.org
- summerhillschool.co.uk

You can find a list of democratic schools here:
- educationrevolution.org
- eudec.org
- democraticschools.directory

*W*e don't have to make human beings smart. They are born smart. All we have to do is stop doing the things that made them stupid.

—John Holt

YOUR KIDS' UNIQUENESS IS THEIR GREATEST STRENGTH

MANY PARENTS AND MISGUIDED TEACHERS think that you should focus on fixing a child's weaknesses by spending more time, attention, and money on the subject in which the child gets the worst grades to create a well-rounded, educated kid. However, it is actually better to focus on their strengths.

Dear reader, focus on your children's strengths instead of their weak skills. Children perform at their best when you empower them to do what they are best at.

Let go of the well-rounded mentality and help your children develop their innate talents. Observe your children, as they will give you clues about their strengths. Once you have an idea of what they are yearning for and what they learn rapidly, as well as when you see them most enthusiastic and fulfilled or when they lose track of time because they are so engrossed, invest in those strengths.

Trying to mold children does more harm than good. Don't mold them into what you think they should be. They are individuals, and they are unique. When you try to develop and manipulate them, you are not allowing the natural process of your children becoming themselves and reaching their full potential. It's like molding and manipulating a cocoon. The butterfly will either die or come out damaged. Why not let the chrysalis take its natural course?

What is strength?

Understanding your children's strengths is an essential aspect of their development. You must consider three key elements to identify their strengths: performance, energy, and use.

Performance refers to activities or subjects that a child excels in. Pay attention to the areas where they perform well and encourage them to pursue these interests further.

Energy is another important factor in identifying strengths. Activities or subjects that leave children feeling energized and motivated will likely be areas of strength. Encouraging your children to engage in these activities can help build their confidence and motivation.

Finally, *use* refers to children's natural inclination towards using their strengths. They will naturally choose to engage in activities that utilize their strengths. As a parent, observing your children and recognizing these inclinations is essential, so you can encourage them to develop these strengths further.

When your children use their strengths, they are highly engaged. They become so engrossed that they lose track of time, show rapid learning curves, exhibit a pattern of repeated success in that area of strength, and perform at above-age-appropriate levels.

When you start noticing a hint of strength in your children, involve them. Provide them with appropriate equipment and label their strengths, letting them know they are good at reading, writing, talking, performing, counting, cooking, sports, drawing, or anything else. Create experiences and an environment that fosters that strength and practice it to develop it further. Connect your children with role models who share the same strength in real life or through biographies in books, websites, or YouTube videos.

Here's an example to help you understand what I'm trying to say. When I noticed my son's strength in playing chess, I enrolled him in a chess club and tournaments, and he practiced chess on the computer. He was so proud of himself. And when I noticed his strength in writing, I kept telling him how good he was at spelling, writing, and editing.

When I observed my daughter's strength in running, I provided her with activities such as running clubs, track meets, and cross-country events, and she thrived. When I saw her strength in reading, I kept finding books for her and telling her what a fantastic, avid reader she was.

When I noticed my youngest son's strength in sports, I enrolled him in various sports. Everyone kept telling us he was the MVP. And when I discovered his strength for inventing delicious recipes, I provided him with all the necessary ingredients and gave him freedom in the kitchen. He felt so intelligent and independent.

Parents who used to focus on their children's weaknesses and shift their focus to strengths report that their children are more motivated, valued, and have more fun. Instead of improving children's weak skills, this approach offers hope for promoting happiness and achievement by developing their character. As their strong skills improve, you will also notice improvements in areas where they previously struggled. Cultivate your children's natural tendencies, skills, and interests so they are more inclined to experience accomplishments. If you want them to succeed, you will need to take their unique qualities, which are beautiful and powerful, seriously.

Strengths give your children energy and make them feel dynamic. You'll see them lose track of time because they focus on areas where their strengths shine. Making your children focus on their weaknesses drains their energy. It makes them tired, affecting their ability to concentrate and inhibiting their learning progress. Have you noticed how exhausted kids are when they come home from school?

Focus on their strengths and avoid comparing them with others. Celebrate their unique abilities and help them grow even stronger.

The human animal is a learning animal; we like to learn; we need to learn; we are good at it; we don't need to be shown how or made to do it. What kills the processes are the people interfering with it or trying to regulate it or control it.

—John Holt

DESCHOOL MAKES EVERYTHING COOL

TO EDUCATE YOUR CHILDREN SUCCESSFULLY, you must give them autonomy to self-direct their learning. To do that, you need to not replicate school at home. Instead, unschool.

Unschool is a word that John Holt used in trying to communicate to homeschool families to not replicate school at home, to avoid the educational errors schools were making, and to emphasize that kids learn better out in life, precisely because it is not school at all.

To fully allow children to lead their education, you must deschool and drop the schoolish thinking. You must work on changing your mindset if you want to educate successfully. I mentioned early that some of us unschoolers try to forget the school patterns, rhythm, and standards because we want our children to learn naturally, following their curiosity and what interests them.

It is challenging to educate your children freely if you

still have a school mindset. And it is challenging to be a facilitator (teacher) in a democratic school if you don't stop acting like a school teacher. If you change your way of thinking, your life will change, too—for the better!

Reset. Restart. Refocus.

To stop thinking like the authoritarian school and to allow your children to follow their path at their own pace, you must deschool your mind. Once you erase the school mentality, everything your kids do will look cool because you'll understand your kids are learning. You'll calm down and let your children do what they need to do to learn their own way.

Deschooling is difficult for many adults who grew up going to school. It is tough to get rid of such ingrained culture in us. Why was it easy for me? In my case, I read all John Holt's books, one by one, in the order he wrote them. Since he worked as a teacher and I did too, it was easy for me to relate. Everything Holt wrote made sense to me as an educator, and it also made sense as the young student I once was.

That may be why these books helped so much to deschool my mind. The kid in me and the frustrated teacher in me agreed with every single word Holt wrote. However, many parents read John Holt and still are not convinced that letting children learn without copying the school method is the best way to learn. Deschooling is different for everyone. Other parents learned from other authors. More information has come out over the years. Doctors in psychology have written articles, essays, and books about the benefits of self-directed education. I encourage you to read Peter Gray, Naomi Fisher, Gina Riley, Sandra Dodd, and Kerry McDonald.

It was easy to remove the school mentality from my mind because I was a great example of a person who was taught knowledge, yet I knew nothing.

A few reasons that helped me deschool include:

- I was taught to read in school, yet I never read. I cheated on every book report.
- I was taught to write in school, yet I was never good at it and avoided it like the plague. I was and still am terrible at spelling. After years and years of memorizing the correct spelling and its rules, I still forget.
- I was taught math in school, and I was good at it, yet I had no idea how to determine twenty percent off while shopping at the store or how to calculate a tip.
- I was taught history in school, my worst nightmare. I never remember anything about my country's history. It's pathetic.
- I was taught science in school. I loved and understood it and saw its value and importance. However, when it was time to explain to my daughter why a solid item can go through water, I remembered learning something in school about molecules. Still, I wasn't able to explain it.

It is so obvious to me through my own example that

the school, despite their best intentions, didn't educate me successfully.

Another example that helped me deschool and trust self-directed education was my experience, noticing how easy and efficient learning was when I followed my interests and needs. I learned more once I was out of school and college than when I was a student in it.

After college, which I learned nothing from (I'm not kidding), I left my country and started an adventure in the U.S. To be allowed to stay in the U.S. longer than a tourist and to be able to work required a large number of hours searching on the internet for rules, laws, paperwork, and what options I had. I did this research before Google existed, when the internet was brand new to us, in 2000.

Once I arrived in the U.S., I was hired as an assistant teacher in a child development center. I learned greatly by observing teachers, kids, and their interactions. When I moved from the suburbs to the city of Atlanta, my curiosity struck. Why was almost everybody black in the city and white in the suburbs? Why are some schools ninety-nine percent black kids and some schools are only white? I deep-dived into HISTORY. I, the hater of the most boring subject, voluntarily started reading and asking questions to my black coworkers, learning, understanding, and retaining the information. I learned about black history and native Americans and took a deep dive into the history of South Africa. That's when I realized you can't learn what teachers teach you. You learn when you are curious, can relate, and when it makes sense to learn it. I wasn't a bad history student. I didn't hate learning history. The education system I grew up with was flawed.

When I was hired as a kindergarten teacher, I spent the whole summer before starting the job studying and reading books on how and what to teach five-year-olds. I went to college to study education, got my degree, and had no idea how to teach a kindergarten class. I've never learned as much as I did that summer. Two months of independent study deep diving into kindergarten education taught me more than a few years in college.

I can go on and on with all the things I learned because I was interested, curious, or it was a need. But the point is, I completely understood that I learned more on my own than when I was a student in a school. I experienced what my kids would do if I allowed them to learn independently.

And finally, what helped me completely deschool my mind one hundred percent was witnessing my six-year-old start to read books without any reading instruction. After that, I started to see more learning while my children were free to play. My son enjoyed memorizing maps, countries, and their flags. My daughter enjoyed reading animal books nonstop and insanely learning facts. My older son started to learn history and politics for pleasure. It was a beautiful sight. I was completely starstruck.

Some of you were good students and remember what you learned in school. Maybe that is why you have a hard time deschooling your mentality. But ask yourself: *Do you have any passions? Are you deeply interested in something?*

Do you like your job and your life? I met many adults who were good students and are now numb and don't know what they like. Coerced education diminished their creativity, interests, and passions.

Let go of the idea that humans only learn and do things when instructed by someone else, and look at education with fresh eyes. Young children are constantly curious. Are you? Do you stop and look with amazement at what is in front of you? Adults in your life exercised control over your learning and killed the joy you had of learning. We are all programmed to learn and grow. Go back to viewing the world through a child's eyes, and you'll see how much learning there is in one day.

Many parents think if they don't make their kids learn, they won't choose to learn. Others say their kids are lazy and disinterested. When you allow a person the freedom to learn what they want, when they want, they come to learning with fierce passion and energy. Children who seem not to have any interests grew up without autonomy and were not allowed to follow their curiosity. Those kids will gain their curiosity and interests back when you give them the freedom to explore, try things, do activities, and think independently.

Some parents worry that their kids will have gaps. And the thing is, everyone has gaps. Everyone! Kids that learn freely are not ashamed of having gaps. It's part of their lives. When they encounter some situation they do not know how to handle, they find a resource to figure it out. They are clever. They will ask an expert, Google it, find a documentary, read about it—you name it, they'll do it to find the answer. The gap will be filled soon enough.

Focus on what's most important—your children and their learning. Instead of wondering what school children are learning (try to tune out when school parents are talking), redirect your attention to what interests them, what brings them joy, and what you could do to help them explore. Over time you'll learn to loosen your teaching expectations and trust your kids, letting them guide their learning more and more.

Deschooling is also removing any hopes of a preset career for your children and accepting what comes, accepting every career without judgment. Don't judge jobs and careers by how important they sound to brag to friends and family. Let's judge a job and career by how happy our children are by seeking it. If your child's passion is to become a dancer and you were hoping your kid would become a lawyer or a doctor, accept the dancing career without judgment. When you embrace self-directed education, you must accept every outcome with neutrality. Is this what's holding you back?

I reassure you that home-educated children and self-directed school students can graduate from college, start a business, get jobs, live creative lives, and become independent adults. Some take nontraditional learning paths right through their teen years and into adulthood; others begin taking community college classes as teens or work with mentors.

This education method offers more than a different way to get the same results as others. You won't know your destination, but it will be the perfect destination for each of your children.

Self-directed education is the only education that genuinely works. And by *work*, I mean children really learn. It prepares them for real life while being in it. Once you witness the beauty of children learning independently, you enter a whole new world. And you won't want to return to traditional school methods; it will seem strange. Why do they separate kids by age and limit their interactions to short recess periods? Children are forced to socialize with children only their own age and are trapped in a room for hours. They divide learning by subjects and must learn what's in the schedule without respecting their curiosity. How horrible is it for a student fascinated by science to spend time learning language arts?

Do you think school is a safe bet for your kids' successful future? I recommend you stop thinking of the future. If you focus entirely on the children who are here now, you will give them everything that they need to become the adults they want to be. Don't let beliefs and cultural programming dictate your life. Let go of what traditional education looks like, follow the interests of your children, and meet their unique learning needs. Design your life based on your values and your kids' values, purpose, and aspirations.

Many children suffer because their education does not account for them as people. What is education for? Who is it for? The most important lessons anyone learns in life are not learned from an educator's well-thought-out, curated lesson plan. They are learned from life itself.

Embrace not knowing what your children are learning by being interested in specific topics and getting engrossed in particular activities. Trust that it is precisely what your children need for their development.

Live your life. Allow your children to live their lives. Play until your body says no more. Enjoy the whole week like every day is another Saturday. And erase the school-like thoughts. Try it. You'll be amazed. Focus on the present moment rather than worrying about the future. Experience life as it unfolds. You don't know what the future will look like.

Believe in your children. Have faith in their abilities. Without confidence in them, they can't be successful.

Remember: It is impossible not to learn.

Misconceptions

1. Teachers are the only ones qualified to teach, especially in certain subjects like math and science.
2. Children must be in a school building five days a week for years to learn and socialize.
3. Children must always be told what to do and be supervised.
4. You must learn certain things at a certain age.
5. Children must be grouped by age.
6. Grades and tests are essential.
7. Play is not necessary. It is an extra activity for after finishing schoolwork.
8. Parents and students have little say in the decisions made about learning.

9. Compliance with coercion is good and produces responsible citizens.

TRUTHS

1. Children can co-learn by taking turns guiding, teaching, facilitating, and learning, depending on their expertise, temperament, and circumstances.
2. Learning occurs naturally at all times and in all places.
3. Children need to have the option to join groups or be alone, depending on their preferences. However, there may be instances when younger individuals require the protection and guidance of older co-learners to ensure their safety and acquire valuable knowledge.
4. Children can learn what they want when they need or desire to do so.
5. Children benefit profoundly from working and playing with people of all ages.
6. The most effective ways for learners to track their progress include self-evaluation, reflection, and constructive feedback. However, there may be instances where learners opt to use grades and tests as valuable tools to assess their progress.
7. Playing is the natural way in which humans learn.
8. Students and their families must have the primary say in their learning decisions.

9. The most effective way to cultivate responsible citizens is through the principles of freedom and democracy.

Here are some books that can help you deschool your mind:
1. *How Children Learn* by John Holt
2. *The Unschooling Handbook* by Mary Griffith
3. *Dumbing Us Down: The Hidden Curriculum of Compulsory Schooling* by John Taylor Gatto
4. *Free to Learn* by Peter Gray
5. *Unschooled: Raising Curious, Well-Educated Kids* by Kerry McDonald
6. *Why Are You Still Sending Your Kids to School?* by Blake Boles
7. *An Unschooling Manifesto* by Marla Taviano
8. Unschooling Rules by Clark Aldrich
9. *Sage Homeschooling: Wild and Free* by Rachel Rainbolt

These are just a few. There are many, many more, so look for the book that speaks to you!

Schools assume that children are not interested in learning and are not much good at it, that they will not learn unless made to, that they cannot learn unless shown how, and that the way to make them learn is to divide up the prescribed material into a sequence of tiny tasks to be mastered one at a time, each with its appropriate "morsel" and "shock." And when this method doesn't work, the schools assume there is something wrong with the children— something they must try to diagnose and treat.

—John Holt

INTERESTS ARE POWERFUL

INTERESTS ARE SUBJECTS, IDEAS, THINGS, topics, and events that fascinate and stimulate your children's curiosity. What seems like an obsession with a particular subject, book, animal, or sport will provide a major leap pad for further learning. Any interest—from the common to the most bizarre (who are we to label it bizarre?)—will be the perfect motor to keep your child learning.

The power of interest drives learning. Your children learn more effectively when you engage them in everyday activities based on their interests. Interests help them think more clearly, understand more deeply, and remember more accurately.

To gather information about your children's interests, you should observe your children throughout the day in as many activities as possible.

Once you know your children's interests, you can include them throughout the day to take advantage of all the learning opportunities. But avoid turning their interests into a lesson. You'll destroy that interest fast. Follow your children's lead. Let children show you and tell you what fascinates them about their interests. Kids will open up about their interests and talk about them nonstop. You will not need to test them to find out if they are learning.

For example, when a child is fascinated by ants, reads books about them, memorizes the names of each type and the duties of the queen and workers, Googles what they eat and other info, watches videos of where they live, and tells you all about it, there is no need to sit down and make that child do a project, essay, or test about what they learned. They are learning! The child thinks they are playing, because searching for information about their favorite topic is indeed playing. Still, you will see that they are actually learning. As I told you earlier, these two words, *playing* and *learning*, are the same.

My son was obsessed with world maps, atlas, countries, capitals, mountains, rivers, and buildings. He learned and memorized much information by playing (looking, observing, studying, exploring) maps. While having fun following his interests, he learned a great deal. There was no need to test him on his geography skills. It was obvious.

Using children's interests and everyday activities at home provides many more learning opportunities than is possible during school. Kids are motivated to learn. Your children are more likely to pursue their passions than other topics they're not excited about. It's much easier to encourage learning about history, science, or math for children who are already interested in the subject.

By encouraging their passions and interests, you're also helping children do well in other areas. You are making them feel understood by supporting their interests, no matter how off-beat or different they might be. Your support and encouragement remind them how loved they are, no matter what.

How to support their interests

Find books, videos, websites, museums, and workshops about the topic. Give toys, materials, or a kit about the topic. Ask questions and listen. Listen without judgment. And don't correct too quickly, even if they have their facts wrong. They'll learn them in due time.

Following your children's interests can lead to so many amazing learning experiences you would never have thought to explore. But do not mistake following your children's interests with forcing your lessons and topics of study. There's no need for lessons when kids are already learning. Remember, your kids are in charge. Kids can follow their unique interests, curiosity, and imagination to learn many amazing things. They learn things because they see the value in them. To give a successful education, let children lead the learning.

Your children's interests will cover reading, writing, and math. If, for some reason, after following your kids' interests, math has not been learned, you will notice that your kids learn math just by living life because, in our everyday life, math is all around us. (What time is it? How many minutes in the microwave? The speed limit on the highway, the money you make and spend, shopping, the temperature, ounces, inches, pounds, and yards . . . math is everywhere!)

I can't emphasize this enough—do not turn their interest into a lesson. Don't ask them to write a story about their interest or to read and comment on an article, make a presentation, or summarize a book. While your kids are soaking up all the information about their obsession, they are learning deeply and truly. Your worry about needing to practice reading and writing (you need to deschool, remember?) is ruining their beautiful, natural learning. Do not interrupt the flow. There might or might not be reading and writing involved. Maybe there will be YouTube watching and zero reading, but trust me. Eventually, your children will read and write.

If possible, give children uninterrupted time to follow their ideas and interests. This will result in a much greater progression of ideas. Provide resources and all kinds of possibilities for their learning environment. For example, let them spend all morning playing in the bathtub full of water using straws, measuring cups, and colanders, even though it is not bath time. Let them set up the camping tent in the living room with all their toys and books, and spend a few nights in it, even though camping tents are for camping. Let them go on with their ideas. As long as they are not harmful to anyone, these ideas will lead to other ideas, and those other ideas will lead to more learning. Don't stop the process.

Some children will be motivated to learn through easily recognized patterns and methods. Others will learn and express their ideas differently through imaginative play, building and constructing, painting, or daydreaming. Some parents and educators are skilled in interpreting what children are learning and how they learn best, but others don't and panic. Trust that when you see your kids doing something that doesn't seem educational, it actually is. Trust them and follow their lead.

Here are some reasons to follow children's interests in case I haven't convinced you yet:

- If children are interested, they will learn.
- Confidence and self-esteem will be raised if a child's interests are followed.
- Development in all academic areas can be achieved by following a child's interests.
- Each child is an individual and should be seen this way.
- Knowing and supporting your children's interests creates a good relationship and bond, which are crucial for development in the early years.

Some parents have asked me, "How do we encourage children to pursue their interests if they don't have any?"

Start by exposing them to everything around you. For example, do activities that interest you. Take your kids to explore what you are interested in. Combine it by also going to activities in your city or town you live in. Go to your nearby library, museum, recreational, and sports center. Go for a walk at your closest natural park, mountain, river, lake, or beach. Think like a tourist and visit what a tourist would in your city. Or sit on your couch and browse documentaries online to see what interests you both. By living everyday life and enjoying unstructured free time, interests will surface. Your job is to put your children in situations where they will learn.

Another way to discover what interests your children is by providing free play. Lots and lots and lots of free, uninterrupted play will develop their interests. Once those interests emerge, give your children free time to explore them. When you give free time for them to be productive, they'll have a better chance at figuring out what they're really interested in.

Find activities that will allow them to explore their interests more. Use books, podcasts, movies, documentaries, clubs, magazines, and classes. Let them interview someone. But don't push them. Remember, you can offer, provide, and ask, but your children need to be in the driver's seat when pursuing their interests. If you tell them how they should pursue their interest, you can squash their passion and make it seem more like schoolwork than anything else. To encourage them to continue exploring what they like, allow your children to work at a comfortable pace.

Give them the tools they need and always offer the resources your children need to really dive into their passions.

I've often been asked, "But what if something is essential, and they are not interested? How are they going to learn it?"

The keyword here is "essential." If something is absolutely necessary, your children will learn it. And if something is highly important to you but not essential, they will inevitably be exposed to it because you will talk about it and show it to them. They might not become experts, but they will be exposed.

Think for a moment about what you mean by "essential." It's *crucial* not to cross the street when cars are driving by, and of course, we all teach that to our kids. Paying for the items you buy at the grocery store is important, and we teach our kids by modeling. It's vital to brush your teeth daily, clean the dishes after you cook and eat, not touch fire or hot water, and close the doors and windows when it's cold outside. All these important things will be learned because you will model them daily.

Do you mean *essential* things like knowing who Cervantes is, who painted the Mona Lisa, the names of important philosophers, geography, and their country's history? If your children are unwilling to learn what you plan for them, they won't learn it. As simple as that. They might memorize it to please you or cheat to get out of it. You can't force learning; it occurs spontaneously, and you can't coerce it. But you can undoubtedly expose children to what's important to you.

Listen, your children will learn important things if those things are in their lives. They will learn and talk about your history if you are proud of it. Invite them to come with you when an art exposition comes because you would love to show them great art (don't make it into a lesson, only exposure). Bring home classic books by great writers and talk about them during supper. Don't force your children to read these books. Just introduce those books so your children know they exist.

Suppose you think something is *essential* that must be learned. You don't see your kids learning it at all. In that case, expose them or wait until they are older, around high school age, and have a meaningful conversation with them. Let them know why you think it's important to gain that specific knowledge.

For example, when my son was about to turn eighteen years old, he had not studied math since he left fourth grade. Of course, he learned all the math that can be learned by living life, and since he pursued a writing career, he didn't need algebra or AP calculus. So, I never forced him to learn advanced math. However, I told him that it would make me feel better and more responsible as a parent if he took a practical math class. This teaches you about taxes, banks, credit, budgeting, and house buying. These skills can be learned by listening, observing, practicing, and emulating the adults around us. But my husband and I could have been better role models in that subject. I told my son I didn't want him to be like me or his dad. He understood, and it made sense to him to take a practical math class.

It is imperative for success that the student initiates the learning. Hold the urge to tell your children what they have to learn. Do not pressure children to learn a particular subject you think is essential. The entire responsibility is left to the student. Of course, you can offer and share information with kids by saying something like, "Hey, this semester, the library offers this class. Do you want to take it?" Or "I found out about this web page called Coursera. They have a lot of online college classes there." Or, "This mom enrolled her kid in that class. Do you think it's cool? Are you interested?" You can offer all you want, but let it go if they are uninterested.

Are you afraid that if children are left to their devices, they will never learn anything? Remember, you think like that because you still need to deschool your mind. Forget that children must be told what is important to learn and when to learn it. Students know what is important for them to learn. They are responsible for choosing their interests and, eventually, their life goals. Do you think they want to fail? Of course not. They want the best for themselves. If something is essential for their educational path, to be able to succeed in the future that they have planned, they will learn it.

To give a successful education to your children or students, you must understand that everybody doesn't need the same education. Similarly, everybody needs different resources to achieve success.

Remember, let children be children and do their primary job—PLAY.

Here's an example of my three kids' interests and where they led:

First kid: Trains and cars, *Thomas the Train*, ocean animals, weapons, reading, Playmobil, LEGOs, archery, history, politics, current events, video games, and science led to him becoming a novelist.

Second kid: Diego and his jaguar, cats, dogs, rats, horses, reading, animals, music, piano, violin, flute, composing music, more animals, cooking, more music, more books, running, tree climbing, rock climbing, horse riding, academics, medicine, and aerial circus arts led to her going to college in Europe to further her education as an aerialist athlete.

Third kid: Balls and cars, sports, blocks, maps, Playmobil and LEGOs, more sports, reading, music, climbing trees, running, gymnastics, horse riding, video gaming, building, Minecraft, math, cooking, and soccer have led him to enroll in public school to get a better soccer training opportunity and led him to start investing money, stock trading, and becoming financially savvy.

Of course, all those interests were combined with my interests (swimming, pool days, beach trips, travel, museums, movies) and everyday life.

All three of my kids are happy with their life paths.

The writer wants a quiet, stress-free life. His definition of success is putting his imaginary world on paper for readers to enjoy. And a publishing company wanting to work with him is my definition of success.

The aerialist athlete wants to fly on all kinds of apparatus. She wants to work for Cirque du Soleil and travel worldwide with them. To her, working and being surrounded by talented athletes defines success. To me, the fact that being a circus artist is a well-paid job and a fun life to live is a success.

The soccer player wants to be free, never work nine to five, and never worry about money. To him, success is being financially savvy to support his lifestyle. He's proud of his achievements and is aware that a soccer career could not pan out, but his investments are growing, which is a success to me.

Encouraging your children to be who they are is one of the biggest learning resources you can provide. Everyone learns differently and has interests in different things. By encouraging those interests, you're setting your child up for a lifetime of greater success.

Your children's interests may change, and it's okay to let them quit when they are no longer passionate about pursuing them. It's important to remember that quitting is not always bad. Trust and support.

Children do not need to be made to learn about the world, or shown how. They want to, and they know how.

—John Holt

THE IMPORTANCE OF FREE PLAY

NATURE CREATED A PROCESS TO ALLOW OUR complex human brain to develop itself: play.

Most people find it hard to believe that our children's lifelong success depends on their play. They think play is a useless way to pass the time, a waste of time, or a treat for working hard. But play is much more than that. It is the learning language of children. Don't silence it.

Play is a range of intrinsically motivated activities for recreational pleasure and enjoyment. But don't get confused. Pleasure and joy are not disassociated from work. Work is not the opposite of play. Play can also be as structured and as serious as work.

Play unlocks many physical, mental, social, and emotional benefits in children and adults. Besides the obvious benefit of a healthy body and improved motor skills, better flexibility, increased balance, and coordination, it also gives us healthier minds.

Play promotes brain growth, especially of the cerebellum (responsible for motor control) and hippocampus (thought to be the center of emotion and memory, especially long-term memory). It also leads to the development of divergent thinking (the ability to develop many independent solutions to the same problem).

Periods of unstructured free play often lead to new types of games with rules made up as they go, improving creativity and enhancing productivity. Kids who enjoy their work and daily work feel more engaged. This translates to higher morale and the propensity to work harder.

Free play gives children better social, emotional, and self-regulation skills, along with a sense of belonging. It improves emotional intelligence and helps build confidence and the ability to work well in groups.

Spontaneous play reduces stress and anxiety. Engaging in play boosts coping strategies and leads to an improved outlook on life. Periods of unstructured play often provide opportunities for children to share, negotiate, resolve conflict, and reach a consensus, which makes them better people.

Play provides opportunities for fostering children's curiosity. Without curiosity, kids can't learn. Play deprivation is not only associated with the increasing prevalence of attention deficit/hyperactivity disorder, but it is also abuse.

Let them play.

Play is the work of children. It is their natural way of learning, exploring, trying, and practicing. Play will lead your children to advanced learning, deep searching, engrossed exploring, and—believe me when I say it—their future jobs.

Your kids will not know the difference between play

and learning; when they grow up, they will not notice the difference between play and their careers.

Free, unstructured, self-chosen play is the train your children need to hop on to stay on track and not get lost on the way to their successful future lives.

I think the teaching of reading is mostly what prevents reading. Different children learn different ways. I think reading aloud is fun, but I would never read aloud to a kid so that the kid would learn to read. You read aloud because it's fun and companionable. You hold a child, sitting next to you or on your lap, reading this story that you're having fun with, and if it isn't a cozy, happy, warm, friendly, loving experience, then you shouldn't do it. It isn't going to do any good.

—John Holt

READING INSTRUCTION IS THE ENEMY OF READING

I COULDN'T AGREE MORE WITH JOHN HOLT when he said, "I think reading instruction is the enemy of reading."

I learned to read when I was a young kid in school. The ability to decode every single word in a book wasn't difficult, but I never enjoyed reading. I never understood why reading was fun to some people. The books we read as a whole class were BORING. And teachers never tried to find a book I might be interested in.

I did not like reading until my twenties when a friend who knows me very well suggested I try a romance author he knew would be perfect for me. I devoured all the books this author wrote. That's when I realized I love reading! I just didn't like the books the school assigned us to read. I spent years reading romances, one after another, enjoying reading like never before. Then I got curious about memoirs, then dystopia. When there were no more books for me to read, I got curious about popular best-sellers that everyone talked about. I liked reading them too! Then self-help books, parenting books, and books about education. I became a bookworm.

I'm telling you this to emphasize the importance of letting children choose what books to read and respect if they are not interested in a book you think it's a must-read. It is more important to let them fall in love with the act of reading than to give them a list of books that must be read, which can sadly confuse the task of reading as boring.

Since I was obsessed with my kids not being like me as a child (I never read a book), I treated books in my home like part of our toys, activities, and routine. I never treated reading like a chore that must be practiced. It was more like a fun activity. Learning to read requires motivation, and loving books provide that motivation for your child.

Buy kids books as presents, take children to the library and encourage them to borrow whatever they like, provide quiet time to read even if they are just studying the pictures, and promote books as precious sources of enjoyment and knowledge.

With that said, let me guide you on helping your kids to learn to read successfully.

Read aloud to your kids from day one. A long time ago, when I started my teaching career, a dear veteran teacher told me, "Read, read, read, and one day the kid will read back to you." And now I'm passing this wise message to you, because it works.

Reading aloud is the best thing you can do. Start as soon as you can. Read anything that they want you to. Kids of most ages enjoy picture books. If this task is boring, find somebody to do it for you or use audiobooks. Since I didn't enjoy that task, my husband took over and read to our kids every night before bed.

Teaching reading is not teaching. It is facilitating. It is more about the steps you take to provide the best learning environment for your children. The child is doing all the work. You only provide. You simply supply the tools, the time, and the guidance. The learner does the most important part.

Create a language and literature-rich environment. Place all kinds of books, especially easy-to-read kid-friendly books, atlases, maps, menus, catalogs, magazines, instructions, recipes, and letters or messages from you, where kids play and rest. When the environment is full of print, kids will read while they play because it will be part of their games.

Model reading from left to right and help your child recognize print by pointing out repeating letters and words. Also, point out signs around you, letters in magazines, cereal or pizza boxes, milk or juice cartons, and all around you.

Label objects in your house and your children's rooms, especially to help them organize toys, clothes, and kitchen items. They love to know where to put their toys when it's time to clean up. Write a message near their bed that reads "Good night," "I love you," or their name.

Read repetitive books with similar sounds. Ask your

child to guess what the next word might be.

Another task we adults have to do to facilitate learning to read is to practice and exercise sound awareness. You can do that during the day while you bathe, cook together, or drive.

- Play rhyming games, make up jingles with different rhyming words, and make silly rhymes. (I saw a fat cat. I saw a red bed. I saw a big pig.) Make up endings or change words in rhymes, poems, songs, or short stories that your kid has memorized and see if your children can figure out what you changed.

- Play listening games. Ask your children to close their eyes and identify the sound (crumpling or tearing paper, tapping a table with your fingernails, dribbling a ball, opening a bag of chips, eating celery). You can also make sounds in a sequence and ask your kids to remember the sequence. Remember, these are games to play and have fun, not a lesson.

- Play "Eye Spy" and list objects you can see that start with certain sounds.

- Take out sounds in words and see if your children can identify missing sounds.

- Clap your name, words, songs, and poems with different syllables.

- Practice alliteration by having fun with silly sentences with similar sounds about everyday objects: "Stop singing sad songs" or "Candy can cook coconuts."

•Play around by saying all the voiced and un-
voiced phonemes (/f/: /v/).

When your children are ready, use simple but effective resources and keep it positive. When they're ready,
they'll fly through it, so there's no point forcing reading
early and making it harder than it needs to be. If you start
to help them read and you notice your children struggle
with the basics, put it off for a few months. Wait until
your children are interested and are making progress.

How do you know a child is ready?

If children pretend to read, try to read, or ask for help
reading a word they are interested in, they are ready to
start learning to read. That may happen at age four or
ten. The range is so wide that it creates chaos. The majority of kids start reading when they are five or six, but
many kids read when they are eight, and some don't start
until they are twelve.

Your children are ready to learn to read if they:
• Recognize print as different from pictures in
books
• Ask what signs or words say
• Enjoy lining up toys or creating patterns
• Engage in focused play
• Can "cross the midline" (reach from one side of
their body to the other)

To help children become readers, we need to show
the association of letter shapes with certain sounds.
But don't get too caught up with phonics. Learning the
sounds is not the only way to learn to read. Whether it

is when they are three or seven, at one point or another, they will be ready. Waiting to teach letter recognition is smart. Wait until their minds have had ample time to hear different words and sounds.

Begin with their name letters as they are important to children. For example, if your child's name is Marta, like me, she'll learn all about *M*, *A*, *R*, and *T*. But if your child loves cars or pizza, these words are important too. Use them.

For each letter sound, you can play a variety of activities depending on where you are at that moment. You can draw the letter on paper, in the sand, or in a foggy car window, copy over the letter, and make the letter shape using playdough or a string. You can find many reading opportunities while playing, cooking, and eating. Practice reading and writing by simply tracing your children's names in the flour or the tomato sauce while cooking a pizza. Use veggies and fruit to compose their name on their plate. Or use blueberries or chocolate chips to write a letter on a pancake. So many ideas!

Find the sound in words wherever you look: signs, book titles, books, cereal boxes, and drinks. Play around with magnetic fridge letters, pick the letter out of a group of foam letters, scatter letters on the ground, and have children land only on the sound they are learning. Something as simple as a trip to the grocery store offers many reading opportunities like reading tags, naming veggies that start with a certain letter, and reading letters from magazines or drinks by the cashier.

Make letter books, cut out pictures, and draw

pictures of things that begin with the new sound. Also, every time your kid masters a letter, glue that letter onto their bedroom wall or make a letter necklace. My kids loved playing with plastic foam letters in the bathtub. Each time they picked one up, I made the correct sound.

Once children know their name letters well, introduce the other letters and their sounds. Some reading specialists like to follow this order:

1. s, a, t, i, p, n
2. c, k, e, h, r
3. m, d, g, o
4. l, f, b, q, u
5. j, z, w
6. v, y, x

By teaching the letters in this manner, children can begin forming words very quickly. After learning the first six letters, kids can make words in the "at," "an," "it," "ip," "ap," and "in" word families (fat, rat, bat, cat, bat, and so on). Introducing the letters and encouraging children to begin making words almost immediately creates a huge sense of pride. Starting with lowercase is helpful because so much print in our everyday lives is lowercase, but it's not necessary. Eventually, children learn both upper and lowercase letters. If your kids learn the letters easily, move on to blending sounds (bl, br, tr, cr, st,). Provide ample opportunities for blending the letter sounds together.

Reading is taught alongside writing, so as the new sounds are being learned, they are also being written. But don't make children write if they don't want to.

If they are not ready to write using paper and pencil,

wait for their inexperienced hands to get strengthened by other activities (playing with playdough or LEGOs). They can use any material. Typing letters on the computer or smartphone is also fun. And they can continue using their magnetic, foam, and scrabble letters to form words.

Repetitive books like *Brown Bear, Brown Bear, What Do You See?* are great tools. Children can concentrate on a few new words by repeating the known initial phrase.

Use easy-to-read books with a lot of repetition. Also, use Bob books and anything similar, or you can create your own mini Bob books. Listen to an audiobook and turn the pages at the appropriate time. Make picture books with the newly learned words. And model how you read.

Some kids pick up patterns automatically, and others may need extra help. Some kids rapidly figure out that the letters *T* and *H* together have two different sounds (the, thank you), and some kids need an adult to point it out. Don't have any expectations. When children run on their own schedule, you must accept that they may not read until they are much older than you want them to.

Phonics (the letter sounds) is not the only way to learn reading. Kids need other skills too. Other activities we need to help our kids become readers are sequencing, writing, meaning (semantics), and comprehension.

Sequencing is the order of the letters.

You can play games on how to put the letters of words correctly. For example, going back to my name, to spell Marta, you can't write Mtraa. The letters have to be in the correct order. Have fun playing with easy words first. Easy words are consonant-vowel-consonant, for example, cat, rat, bat, dog, dot, pot, pig, big, red, and bed.

Children must learn to read words organized to convey meaningful messages to become readers. Children need to work with words and sentences that mean something. You can create a personalized book (nothing fancy, use paper and pen). For example, give it the title *I Like to Eat*, and on each page, write things your kid likes to eat:

I like to eat bananas.

I like to eat ice cream.

I like to eat chocolate.

I like to eat pizza.

And I don't like carrots.

Reading personalized books will have more meaning than reading about what a fake character likes to eat. Personalized learning increases student motivation and engagement. You can create many mini books like, for example, *My Family*:

I have a mom.

I have a grandma.

I have two brothers.

I have one dog.

I have three uncles.

Children love reading if they can read the messages on the printed page easily and effortlessly and see how ideas are put together to create meaningful stories. Children need to comprehend the main idea conveyed by the books to really read. If reading is frustrating and not fun, leave it—don't force it. Then return to easier books.

"What happens if a child doesn't want to learn to read?" Next to learning math and how to write, this is one of the most common concerns.

No such thing happens. In our society, reading is an important communication tool. People are inherently motivated to expand their ability to communicate, and this inherent motivation will result in children wanting to learn to read. Reading is part of our culture. If you read, if everyone around your kids reads, and there is reading material in their environment, children learn to read and largely teach themselves to read because they want to participate fully in society.

Your kids will naturally learn. As long as your environment is rich in literacy, your kids will be interested, bathe in it, and start learning with your help.

Learning to read is a unique experience for each child. Some kids learn the sounds of letters and learn to read easy words like cat, fat, and rat. Some kids learn to read by memorizing words or an easy-to-read book with pictures that help them guess. I even met families whose kids learned to read by watching TV with subtitles or playing video games.

The best thing to understand how to teach reading is to not stress about it! It will happen. Relax, and don't force it. If you push it when kids are not ready, you can place incredible pressure on their shoulders, block them, and harm their natural process.

Please don't worry if you find everything you read in this chapter intimidating. If this is too much information or it seems daunting, know that plenty of websites and apps can help. Suppose you are not a fan of the internet for young kids. In that case, most libraries have tablets without internet access and apps already downloaded for your kid to learn letters, words, and reading. They also have lots of DVDs for kids to learn reading. Starfall.com, Readingeggs.com, and Readingkingdom.com have become household favorites.

To help your children learn to read, you can also hire a reading tutor, a teacher, or another homeschooling mom. You are not alone.

Families panic when they realize every kid is reading but theirs. It's such an important milestone that worry starts to creep in, causing parents to forget that every child's natural timeline looks different. Remember that some kids learn to read as soon as the adult stops putting pressure and they feel relaxed. Some kids learn to read when the adult chooses to switch to a different reading program. And some kids learn to read when their parents purchase a dyslexia reading program because they suspect their kid has dyslexia. Some schools use the Orton Gillingham Reading Program for all children to avoid learning difficulties. That is something to consider if you are worried. And don't forget to go to the eye doctor for a check-up.

Once children are readers, they need a choice in what they read. It is one way they will become engaged in the text. Kids who do not have a choice may not become good readers. You only become a good reader by reading. Anything counts—reading the back of the cereal box, a toy catalog, a comic, a silly children's magazine, or a recipe card.

Learners naturally find they love to read when they choose their reading materials. When students are forced to read books they dislike or boring text in a workbook, their passion for reading can decline. Allowing children to choose what to read encourages them to enjoy reading independently. It improves comprehension, vocabulary, and fluency and builds confidence in making their own decisions. When kids and adolescents can choose reading materials, they have more ownership in their education and prioritize reading.

"But I don't want my children to read garbage and bad literature."

I have heard many parents say this.

If you want to pass a love of reading to your children, you have to allow them to have joy when they read. This sometimes means reading books that, to you perhaps, are bad literature, but a quality book is one that a child wants to read.

"But how do I get my kids to read?"

Offer books that you think they might like. Model reading. Talk about books. Place books in easy-access places—in their play areas, near their beds, the living room, the kitchen, and your car. And take books with you in your purse. Go to the library and bookstores. And keep in mind that you don't always have to offer books. You can provide magazines, catalogs, menus, poems, recipes, or anything else with words.

When kids are free to self-select books or other reading material, they develop their identities as readers. It's part of an education that teaches them how to think, not what to think. I know you want to tell them what to read, and you can offer and explain why you think the book is so good, but don't force it.

I used to take my kids to a bookstore that was friendly to children, and the books were easy to access. My kids would walk around, grab a book, and read it there. Taking note of their preferred genres, I would look for similar books at the library. On another day, we'd go to the library to get the books I put on hold I thought they'd like, plus the extra ones they chose for themselves. You can always suggest books, magazines, articles, or anything else, as long as you respect their answer.

When you force kids to read, they'll find a way to cheat and pretend they read it. Nobody wins. But suppose you let go of control over what they should read. In that case, children connect with meaningful reading materials and experience greater reading achievement. Their reading skills strengthen, and fluency, comprehension, and vocabulary increase. As reading skills improve, they are more actively involved in learning.

Some books don't speak to us. Kids like books that speak truths that resonate with them. Kids need to find themselves in books and see representation in books that expands beyond their lives. They need the freedom to choose whether they want to read books that are "windows" (books that provide a view into different experiences and perspectives), "mirrors" (books that reflect their own experiences and identities), "roadmaps" (books that offer guidance and inspiration for their own journeys), or pure entertainment. Without that freedom, they might not read at all. I didn't.

One time, I suggested my kids read a book everyone was raving about, *Wonder*, but they weren't interested in it. Months later, I took advantage of a long car trip and told them I would get the audiobook and listen to it. I told them I was curious about the book and wanted to see if I liked it, but they didn't have to listen to it if they didn't want to. We all ended up liking it. You never know! This reminds me—allow your children to not finish a book if it is not grabbing their attention. If they start reading and the author is not keeping them engaged, let the book go and try another one.

There is no need for your children to produce book reports or cute dioramas to prove to you that they read and comprehended the story. You will see how often they enthusiastically share what they read and learn. They want to share what they learn with their siblings, friends, and you, and they gain a desire to know more about the topic they chose. You'll see they love to discuss their chosen reading materials. Don't kill that enthusiasm by assigning a book report.

Students who engage in reading a diverse list of topics and genres lay the foundation for learning. Choosing their reading material gives students a greater desire to dive deep into reading for a lifetime. Students also assume more ownership in their learning when they have a choice and feel more motivated to explore reading materials that can benefit their learning in the future. But do not panic if your kids are not readers. Your kids will read whatever is necessary to follow their dreams and function in society. But it's all right if a person doesn't enjoy reading books or articles. If your children are not book readers, everything will be okay. There are other ways of learning and staying informed. Documentaries, podcasts, conferences, auditing classes, and many more resources are fantastic ways of learning.

Remember, children learn to read when they want to learn to read. Help them do it if they want help.

Here are a few of the many, many reading resources:
- readingeggs.com
- teachyourmonster.org
- hookedonphonics.com
- teachyourchildtoread.com
- starfall.com
- nightzookeeper.com
- pridereadingprogram.com
- homeschoolingwithdyslexia.com
- readingdoctor.com.au

The person who really needs to know something does not need to be told many times, drilled, tested. Once is enough.

—John Holt

DO NOT TREAT WRITING LIKE A CHORE

I HAVE BEEN ASKED NUMEROUS TIMES HOW TO teach writing to children. While I know the exact method that works well, I wanted to confirm it. So, I went straight to the source—my son, who has never received any formal writing instruction—and asked, "Konji, do you remember how you learned to write? People are curious because you write so well, without any formal instruction."

"I just started writing," he replied. As simple as that. The power of natural learning. Children have an innate ability to develop skills without formal instruction.

Children will learn writing as long as they are exposed to print. Like all the other skills and knowledge, children will learn it if we provide the opportunities, the tools, and the exposure. Children learn to write without years and years of drilling spelling and learning to structure sentences. I did not teach my children to write. Instead, they were exposed to all kinds of literature, and all three were avid readers. To them, reading a book was the same as playing and having fun. All that written language was soaked in and integrated, and somehow, my children started to write.

I used this method, too, when I was a kindergarten teacher. I gave my students complete freedom to write or not write whatever they wanted in their journals. I always praised them for their efforts, no matter how simple or misspelled their words were. I found their attempts so precious and would express my happiness and pride to them. Over time, I began to see progress. The children became proud of themselves, their parents were happy with their development, and I was fascinated by the fact that I was not teaching them but simply exposing them to print. The exposure and the freedom to experiment with writing did it all. It's truly beautiful and magical to watch.

Self-directed education has produced three kinds of writers in my family.

My girl, who is 17, only writes when she has to, and she's good at it. She wrote an essay as part of the admission process to get into college without ever having a formal writing class.

My youngest, 15, also writes when he has to and for pleasure. He likes to write in his journal once in a while, and he writes well. He has never had a formal writing lesson, yet he has written numerous essays for his high school homework.

And my oldest, 20, made writing his career and wrote a novel that will soon be published, impressing the publishing editor immensely. His only formal writing instruction was in public school until fourth grade.

How on earth did an unschooled kid become a talented writer? I searched and learned that to be a writer, you need freedom and that instruction kills creativity. The importance of writing is to pass the message, the story. And here's my favorite: Writers learn to write by reading many books and copying their favorite writers.

Not taking language arts classes benefited my son's writing skills. And it blows my mind that my three children don't make spelling mistakes like I do.

Dear reader, do not treat writing like a chore. Instead, expose your children to all writing styles, not only books but also magazines, catalogs, menus, instruction manuals, letters, and more. Have all that material in different areas of the house, where it is easy to reach, especially where they play. I always had pencils, markers, paper, and erasable boards (whiteboards) available. While they played pretend kitchen, restaurant, and store, they wrote. Placing a restaurant menu or a recipe book in their pretend kitchen, a car catalog where they play with cars, a book about buildings where they play with blocks, a calendar and a map where they play can be powerful tools.

Expose children to different styles, techniques, and authors. Every author has unique techniques and methods of writing. Kids learn through imitation. Future writers like to train themselves by copying great literature. Place notebooks around the house—the living room, their bedrooms, and the car. Some kids like journaling. With time they will learn how to narrate stories and express their emotions. They will also perfect their composing skills.

And kids who are not interested in writing will write too. They'll copy the necessary communication formats, like writing messages to their friends. When they grow older, they'll write emails, resumes, cover letters, and whatever else they need. Use keyboards, scrabble, and magnet letters instead of paper for children not interested in writing. They will learn to write if there are alternative, exciting materials.

Read aloud or use audiobooks and discuss. Engage kids in meaningful conversations. Don't discuss in a school-teachery way, but discuss organically. Let it happen naturally. Writing is a conversation on paper. Through talking, they will learn to think and ask questions. Choose books from different genres that children love to read. Let them listen to the texts and learn the sentence patterns and syntax.

It's quite surprising to most parents and teachers that what will turn children into critical thinkers and engaged writers is to not force learning writing skills on kids who are not ready or interested. Writing skills need freedom to be creative to write what pleases and truly motivates the child.

I have seen too many families frustrated because their kids showed lower engagement due to not considering their children's interests. Forced lessons, routine practice, and drill typewriting will diminish interest in authentic, meaningful writing.

Do not treat writing like a chore.

Writing has a lot of stages before it gets to paper or screen. Playing with letters, writing tools, and stories makes children comfortable with writing. Writing is the same as reading to your children before you thought they could read. And just like other milestones, there's no rushing, no matter how badly you or your children wish it would happen. It's important to be aware of these pre-writing activities and give them the space they deserve to develop without rushing kids toward writing. Enjoy the time together, confident that children are developing what they need.

Play with foam letters in the bathtub or swimming pool, write letters on the sand at the beach or park, write letters on the car window when it gets foggy, write letters on the cookie or pizza dough, write letters on the snow, and have fun with those magnet letters on your fridge. Don't make it a lesson, and don't start writing letters to teach. Instead, do it as a game, an art piece, or a message. For example, you can write the first letter of your name and say, "I like my *M* on my name. Do you like your *J* in your name?" and draw a *J*. Or you can write the word *go* and say, "It's easy for me to write *go* because it only has two letters. Other words are very long." Little moments like that teach more than a lesson could.

Model writing, let your children see you write the grocery list or a note to your partner, fill out all the paperwork at the doctor's office, or write an email. When your kids ask you to write a word, do it right there in front of them. Have writing material everywhere in the house.

Trust me, it works—even in the car and your purse.

It is difficult to understand; some of you will roll your eyes. Still, the excitement of telling a story matters more than perfectly formed letters and perfect spelling. The content is what's important. If your kids are not interested in learning letters, they are not ready. Allow them to spend years playing freely. All these unstructured games help them develop stories.

When kids write random letters all over the page and read their "stories" to you afterward, please be proud and encourage your children, because your kids are willingly and excitedly writing stories. It's a great win. It's the beginning of their writing journeys. Those random letters will eventually become misspelled words and eventually real accurate words.

Some kids have such great imaginations and form such great stories that they will ask you to write them. Do it. Write everything they tell you. If they have to write it themselves, it will slow down their creativity. Other kids will show no interest in writing. That's fine. Life eventually will make them write. Like when they go to the doctor and have to fill out paperwork or enter some kind of competition. They have to write their name and other info on a list, or when they want to write something on Minecraft or Roblox or a happy birthday card to a friend.

Don't worry when your friends tell you their kids are creatively journaling non-stop and your kids have zero interest. Your children are simply not interested in sitting down to journal. One kid excels in one area while another is learning a different skill. It's okay if your kids are not writers. They will learn to write when their moment comes, which might be later in their teens. When it's time to learn how to write a cover letter, they will. When their interest leads them to college, they will learn how to write essays.

Avoid handwriting exercises (unless your kid genuinely enjoys them). Relax. Writing will work itself out. Give them time to develop a little more, and never stop presenting other opportunities down the road.

Do not treat writing like a chore.

A successful education nurtures and draws out the writing voices of children without causing damage. Let children express themselves, get in touch with their writing voices, and determine what they want to say and how they want to say it. Establishing their voice and writing process is imperative to fostering the right environment for writing freely. This is how professional writers teach writing.

Teaching writing formats and the structure of writing blocks accessing the words within and sadly creates resentment towards writing. Parents believe children won't write unless we make them and teach them how. Students don't find writing easily if they are told what the shape of writing should be. Giving instructions on format and structure does not help learners express what they want to say.

Don't assign your children to practice writing every day. Let them find out why they need to write. Your kids may need to write an email to someone. They may need to write a review online of a product they are happy or upset about. Maybe they want to write a story. Whatever it is, children must have a need or a reason to write, and when that time arrives, provide help and resources.

As kids get older—middle or high school age—and their writing voices have been cultivated, they'll start to encounter that the classes or courses they willingly asked to be enrolled in demand writing assignments. That's when they'll be ready to learn writing formats. They'll start the quirky process of pulling language from within and finding the best shape. Then they'll polish their writing, revise and edit their work confidently, and share it with others.

When I wrote my first book, I expressed what I had to say as best I could. It was so badly written it was hilarious. Then, like a puzzle, I moved sentences up and down, switched paragraphs left and right, and messed with them. I molded them into a form that reminded me of the memoirs I read. And I learned later that this is exactly how professional writing instruction usually starts—say what you must and edit it later.

Kids who know they can write are ready to tackle any writing assignment as they age, because they feel confident in their powers to generate language and insight. If your children have nothing to say, they won't write. The content has to be meaningful and important to them.

What made me confident not to teach my kids how to write?

Two things. One, I was taught in school and I have only

recently learned to write. The first time I wrote a cover letter, I had to search for a few templates online, and I copied them. And two, friends of mine who are college professors have mentioned to me that most students they have in class (students who graduated high school and started college) do not know how to write.

Now that I have successfully *not* taught my three kids to write, and they can write, I can tell you it works. When you drop the writing instruction and educational plan, you will bolster critical thinking.

Instruction, if not wanted, damages kids' writing.

When you don't use traditional academic methods to teach writing, writing becomes part of real life. When do we ever use academic essay writing? There's often only one purpose behind academic writing. Students are writing for a grade, to pass a class, and to get accepted into college.

Letting go of that mindset builds a new way of thinking. It opens doors for your children's writing they've not thought of before. Writing is a skill they absolutely will use in the real world. They need the opportunity to try it and practice it without being assessed. Effective communication and the sharing of ideas should be the highest priority.

Writing should be a natural part of your day. Immersion is the best way to learn. If you place paper, notebooks, pencils, and markers where children play and in strategic places, you'll start to see scribbles and lines be part of their play. Tell stories and record all the cute things they say. Build comfy writing nooks in the corner of a favorite family room. The more accessible and normal writing is, the better. It's not a shock to the system if you've been doing it all along.

Read and Discuss. Writing is a conversation. What better way to support the development of that skill than through conversation itself? Reading varying genres will not only expose a writer to elements of style, but it will also serve to develop necessary thinking skills. Through discussion, writers learn to ask questions and think critically about them, discovering what they believe and why. And they learn to make comparisons between styles, authors, and techniques.

By being exposed to varied literature across authors and genres, children can analyze the different types of writing and use that as a springboard for their work. They'll better grasp style and grammar through imitation and find their own rhythm. This task is second nature for children because they often imitate through play. They'll build a singular voice and style by listening to the lilt of other literature and then imitating it. It's much more natural than copy work.

Remember, let your kids read everything they can get their hands on first. Eventually, they will write. Help them do it. Don't treat it like a chore.

Suppose your children are interested in learning and improving their writing skills, and you don't feel proficient enough to provide instruction. In that case, you can find classes at your local library, civic center, local community college, outschool.com, coursera.org, or these programs:

- bravewriter.com
- writeshop.com
- essentialsinwriting.com
- essentialsinwriting.com

What can you do if your kid is a poor writer?

Society, in general, confuses the skill of writing with being smart or illiterate, obsessing with making sure kids learn to write well to the point that they harm it. It's important to understand that being a good writer is not a sign of how intelligent you are. Let me explain.

My dad was a fantastic pediatric surgeon, well-known in his field. He became the head of surgeons at the hospital where he worked and even ran for mayor of our city. Although he lost the election, he was offered the responsibility of running the city's health department. And guess what? He is a terrible writer, yet he has written several newspaper articles and saved children's lives.

I went to school where I was taught to write. My parents hired a private tutor because my spelling skills needed to improve. I went to high school, then college, and graduated to become a special education teacher. Years later, I wrote a book and am now writing this one. And guess what? I make spelling mistakes. I don't remember how to spell words I've read and written numerous times.

Spelling mistakes and grammatical errors do not necessarily correlate with intelligence. Teaching spelling and writing skills does not guarantee that you will become a better writer. Smart people can still be bad writers. Some kids are born with better spelling abilities than others. Unfortunately, even with many spelling instructions, some cannot remember the correct spelling.

Thank goodness for spell check! And thank goodness for editors who make you sound wonderful.

Help your children find tools that will help them write better. Not being good at writing shouldn't stop them. Give them tools to manage this "handicap," such as Grammarly.com or ChatGPT, and remind them that editors exist for a reason—to edit our writing.

An editor's job is to review and refine written material before publication. The primary responsibility of an editor is to improve the clarity, accuracy, and coherence of the text they are working on. They do this by correcting spelling, grammar, and punctuation errors and ensuring that the writing flows smoothly and logically. Not being a proficient writer is not a problem.

If writing is too hard for your children and you think they could have a learning disability that makes it difficult to express themselves in writing, check out these websites:

- dysgraphia.life
- ldaamerica.org
- childmind.org
- ghotit.com

Agatha Christie, best-selling novelist of all time, had dysgraphia and dictated her work.

It's a most serious mistake to think that learning is an activity separate from the rest of life, that people do it best when they are not doing anything else and best of all in places where nothing else is done.

—John Holt

MATH

MANY PARENTS ARE CONCERNED ABOUT THEIR
children's math education and wonder how their
children will learn math without being explicitly taught.
It's crucial to remember that your kids will learn what
you use in your everyday lives. Do you add and subtract
in your everyday life? Do you use the Pythagorean
theorem regularly? Whatever math is useful, children will
definitely learn. The advanced math that is not used in
your daily lives will be learned by your children if their
interests lead them in that direction or if they have to
study to pass a test to graduate or attend college. When
that happens, their intrinsic motivation will help them
learn whatever is needed. It only takes them a year to
learn these advanced concepts.

The difference between observing a self-directed
learner adolescent studying high school math to get into
college and a traditional high school student studying
math because it is mandatory is remarkable.

Children naturally learn math, like reading and writing, because they recognize these skills' importance for
survival and success in our culture.

Here's how this learning takes place.

We use numbers every day for practical purposes. We use them to measure things. Give your children the opportunity to use numbers in the same way that you do. Make sure all your measuring instruments are available to your children at easy reach. Let them have fun and explore with measuring tapes, rulers, scales, thermometers, barometers, metronomes, stopwatches, clocks, watches, timers, measuring cups and spoons, and scales. Place a calculator, a few rulers, a watch, a scale, and other measuring tools in their play area.

We also use numbers to count money. Kids are often fascinated by it. They enjoy playing with money, whether when they pretend to go shopping, run a restaurant or ice cream shop, or play a game like Monopoly. Real money is especially exciting for children when they learn that it can buy them a toy, a treat, or a ticket to the movie theater. Money is a great tool for children to learn math. You can use your family's finances as learning opportunities, such as discussing expenses, budgeting for groceries, calculating taxes, understanding insurance costs, and learning about investments. These practical experiences can help children develop essential math skills while gaining knowledge about financial responsibility. Place pretend or real money and foreign money in their play area (avoid giving coins to kids under three as they may put them in their mouth and choke).

Learning math is a part of our life, just like any other part. It shouldn't be turned into a lesson but made accessible to children. The best way for children to learn about numbers is through real-life experiences. Numbers are embedded in our reality—in buildings, highways, cars, velocities, businesses, toys, games, books, music, cooking, and more. Numbers are everywhere in children's lives; they will learn and work with them naturally. Place a calendar, dice, cards, and board games where they play. You'll start to see some math action!

Instead of the traditional approach to math of "Learn math, you'll need it," let children discover why they need math, so they will want to learn it. It makes a huge difference when they want to learn. Children naturally learn to add and subtract when they are ready, and they learn to count and measure when needed. Don't force it. When they approach difficult calculations, they will ask for help or find a way to learn them.

Mathematics is an essential part of our daily lives and has countless practical applications. We use math in many ways, from making calculations at the grocery store to planning a trip, designing a building, or running a business.

One of the most common uses of math is for basic arithmetic operations such as addition, subtraction, multiplication, and division. We use these operations regularly for everyday tasks like budgeting, calculating tips, or measuring quantities for cooking and baking. Because you use it regularly, your kids will be interested and want to learn.

Math is also crucial in science and engineering, where precise measurements and calculations are required for experiments and designing equipment. Math determines measurements, angles, and areas in architecture and construction, ensuring that buildings and structures are safe and structurally sound. And math is a fundamental tool for computer programming, data analysis, and statistical modeling. In medicine, math is used to develop medical imaging technologies, analyze data, and create algorithms for treatment plans. This kind of math will be learned by your children if their interests lead them there. You do not have to be smart in the math department for your children to become mathematicians. Plenty of math tutors, classes, online videos, and online programs will teach your children math without your help.

Mathematics also plays a vital role in finance and economics. It makes projections, calculates interest rates, and analyzes market trends. Business owners and managers use math to determine budgets, forecast revenue, and evaluate profitability. This will also be learned when your kids' interest takes them there. There are online programs, classes, and books that will teach your children financial literacy. My youngest son learned all this because his interest led him there.

Math is a critical part of our daily lives, and its practical applications are numerous and diverse. Whether for personal or professional reasons, understanding and applying mathematical concepts is essential, and your kids will want to learn them to succeed in today's world. If children have no interest in math, they may not pursue academically advanced math. However, they will learn the necessary math skills for daily life. Is that what worries you? As someone who loves math and enjoys solving equations for fun, I have never had to use advanced math in my career or adult life. Despite enjoying finding the value of x, y, and z, and calculating the volume of a prism, the square root of 125, or the missing angle of a triangle, I have never had to use this knowledge in my adult life, nor has my husband and many adults I have asked.

I was not afraid of not teaching math to my children because I love math too much, and I've heard too many people say how much they hate it. Many children in school learn math without fully understanding the concepts they are being taught because teachers focus too much on memorization and rote learning rather than helping students develop a deeper understanding of mathematical principles. When children are simply taught to follow procedures without understanding the underlying concepts, they struggle with applying their knowledge in real-world situations and lose interest in math altogether. This happened to my oldest child. To help your children develop a lifelong love of mathematics and the ability to use math effectively in their daily lives, it is important to avoid forcing concepts on your children. Instead, help them understand math by observing you using it and practicing problem-solving skills in real-life situations.

I do not know the exact time or activity during which my kids learned to count, add, subtract, multiply, and divide. It happened naturally. However, I know how they learned other math facts because they have told me over the years. For instance, they learned about negative numbers by observing the weather temperature. One of my kids learned about angles through photography, another

Math | 119

during aerial acrobat classes, and the third while playing video games. They learned fractions while eating pizza and reading articles in children's magazines that included graphs, pies, and percentages. And they learned about taxes while playing Monopoly.

Learning naturally and self-directed may be difficult to comprehend if you have yet to experience it. Children can discover and use math naturally when math is a normal part of life. It becomes a part of their innate intelligence. They learn the notation when the need arises in the future.

For many, it is hard to see beyond the school mindset because most of us have gone to school. However, unschooling will make sense to you if you focus on what and how your children are learning rather than just on math from a textbook. Waiting for traditional math learning to fit into your lifestyle will only lead to continual disappointment. Suppose you see everything in everyday life as a potential learning opportunity, not just school things. In that case, unschooling will begin to appear effective. Seeing the results firsthand will lead to a newfound belief in this approach.

Here are some examples of mathematics in everyday life.

- Making budgets, managing money, and balancing a checkbook
- Understanding loans for cars, trucks, homes, schooling, or other purposes
- Gardening and landscaping
- Construction projects

- Exercising and training
- Interior designing
- Fashion designing and sewing
- Shopping at grocery stores and supermarkets
- Cooking and baking
- Sports
- Time management
- Driving
- The automobile industry
- Computer applications
- Planning a trip
- Hospitals
- Video games
- Weather forecasting
- The foundation of other subjects
- Music and dance
- The manufacturing industry
- City planning
- Problem-solving skills
- Marketing

Children learn math when they want to learn math.

Help them do it if they want help. If you're struggling to meet their needs, remember there are countless resources at your disposal. Here are a few of them.

- mathantics.com
- khanacademy.org
- unlockmath.com
- ixl.com

- brilliant.org
- mathusee.com
- thinkwell.com
- coursera.org
- And many, many, many more!

Education now seems the most authoritarian and dangerous of all the social inventions of mankind. It is the deepest foundation of the modern slave state, in which most people feel themselves to be nothing but producers, consumers, spectators, and "fans," driven in all parts of their lives, by greed, envy, and fear. My concern is not to improve "education" but to do away with it, to end the ugly and antihuman business of people-shaping and to allow and help people to shape themselves.

—John Holt

AUTONOMY

There are many articles, parenting courses, teacher workshops, and books on how to help children and teens to be motivated. Why are there so many? Why are there so many kids and adolescents not motivated to learn?

Because many kids are told what to do, what to learn, when to learn, and how to learn for years. They have very little autonomy over their lives. That, my dear reader, kills motivation. That is why so many teenagers today are not motivated to learn.

When you closely monitor and control the work and learning of your children, while it may seem like an effective way to ensure productivity and quality, micromanagement can lead to negative outcomes for children and individuals of any age.

One of the primary negative outcomes of controlling is decreased motivation. When children feel like their every move is being watched and evaluated, they become disengaged and less invested in their work. They also feel like their ideas are not valued, which can lead to decreased learning and work satisfaction and an overall lack of motivation to perform well.

Another negative outcome of micromanagement is low self-esteem. When children are constantly being told what to do and how to do it, they begin to doubt their own abilities and feel like they are not capable of making decisions on their own. This can lead to a lack of confidence in their play, learning, or work, negatively impacting their self-esteem.

Finally, controlling can also lead to poor decision-making skills. When children are not allowed to make decisions independently and are constantly told what to do, they may not develop the critical thinking skills necessary to make sound decisions. This can lead to poor decision-making skills that can negatively impact their future.

Not giving children the autonomy they need can have serious negative consequences. You must balance providing guidance and support to your children while allowing them autonomy and independence in their learning and everyday life.

Give them autonomy.

Childhood is a process, allowing children to get to know themselves and what they care about. This process is good for their learning and emotional well-being. Children are naturally curious and want to know everything about the world around them. Giving children the opportunity to be curious and explore their environment is important for their development. Curious children learn and retain information.

Children have the natural instincts to educate

themselves if their environment allows it. Children are designed to explore on their own. They need the freedom to develop. Without it, they suffer.

Suppose you are struggling with educating your children and things are not working well. In that case, you should give them free time and let them try many activities. Eventually, they'll discover their talents and predilections and recover their motivation.

The things children learn through their own initiative cannot be taught in other ways. Successful education is accomplished when students are allowed to be free learners. Forcing activities, manipulating their learning, and micromanaging their future won't lead to success.

Whatever learning system your children choose at any point, it's important to remember that for their education to be successful, you need to respect this consent-based process called self-directed education. When children are free to learn on their own terms, they learn everywhere and all the time. Once you deschool your mind, you'll see learning does not only happen in places and at times set aside for educational purposes.

Remember, the only correct way of teaching is the way that works well for the learner. Kids, teens, and adults learn better when they can choose what they do. Trust in your children's innate ability and motivation to learn. Children and adolescents want to learn, find their paths, and be successful.

Allowing autonomy means letting kids make decisions for themselves. They need the chance to weigh different options, consider alternatives, and think through the outcomes of their choices. Giving them autonomy is crucial for their brains to mature and grow stronger. The best way to learn and practice making good decisions is by starting to make decisions. Are you afraid of your children making the wrong decisions? As a child therapist told me once, it's better for kids to make mistakes when they are young and still live under your roof and protection than when they are older and living independently.

Allowing autonomy means letting children set goals for themselves. When they are young, the goals are usually small. They may want to build a city using blocks, they may want to learn how to play chess, or they may want someone to take them to the zoo. Then the goals will get larger, like getting their first job, buying their first car, or planning their first solo camping trip. Allow your children to learn how to accomplish these goals for themselves. As their confidence grows, so do their goals.

Children and teens lose motivation when you get in their way with doubts, critical tones, and disapproving eyes about what to learn and what career to follow. They conclude there is nothing out there for them. And that's when you will search for an article or a book about how to get that motivation back.

Trust them. Listen and hear what they are trying to tell you. When you support and trust who your children are and know it is not up to you to find their gifts and talents, you'll learn that all they need is the self-confidence to find their way.

A good way to give autonomy and support your kids' decisions is to understand your job is to be there to support their choice and to help them achieve their goals. For example, suppose your children decide that they want to learn a specific subject or pursue a career path. In that case, you can offer to teach that subject or find a class, recommend a book or other reference material, find various resources, or set up an internship program with a local professional. Teens know what they want. Your job is to support and encourage them along their path, but not to determine their path.

Giving autonomy does not mean neglecting your children. It means to give as much freedom as possible inside the parameters of safety and societal rules. Children need the freedom to explore. However, they need to explore in a safe environment. For instance, do not permit three-year-olds to cross a street or swim in a pool without taking adequate safety precautions. Instead, allow them to explore and play in a secure location with as much freedom as possible. As parents and caregivers, establish safety guidelines that help maintain a secure environment. Model these regulations to teach children how to follow them effectively. By doing so, you prevent incidents, such as children getting burned by fireplaces or boiling water, and help instill a sense of safety and responsibility in them.

Do you worry your children will misbehave if you don't control them? Actually, children naturally want to please the adults who care for them. When you build a connection with your children, they'll be more likely to cooperate with you. Misbehavior often stems from a problem that your children are trying to communicate.

Take the time to understand the issue and find a solution for both of you. You'll see that your children follow the rules and behave well when you show respect and foster a mindful relationship.

As an adult, you are responsible for modeling good behavior and demonstrating positive character traits around your children. Kids learn by observing and copying you, so it's important to lead by example. Remember that supporting your children's interests is a great way to connect with them and build a strong relationship. Bad behavior tends to disappear when you have a strong bond, instead of controlling focus on connecting.

Autonomy in learning and development comes with numerous benefits, such as the following:

1. Increased Motivation: Autonomy has been linked to increased intrinsic motivation, meaning that individuals are more likely to engage in an activity because they find it interesting or enjoyable rather than because they are rewarded or punished for doing so.

2. Improved Learning: When individuals have control over their learning, they are more likely to engage in deep learning strategies and retain information better.

3. Higher Achievement: Autonomy has been linked to higher academic achievement, particularly in science, math, and reading.

4. Better Mental Health: Autonomy has been linked to better mental health outcomes, including reduced stress, anxiety, and depression.

5. Increased Creativity: Individuals with autonomy over their learning are more likely to engage in creative problem-solving and innovative thinking.

6. Improved Decision-Making: When individuals have opportunities to make decisions about their learning, they develop better decision-making skills, which can transfer to other areas of their lives.

The negative effects of teacher and parent micromanaging and controlling behaviors in education have been linked to decreased motivation, self-regulation, and academic achievement, along with emotional and behavioral problems in children and adolescents.

Providing your children with more autonomy will benefit their learning and development. It will help them build important life skills such as responsibility, decision-making, independence, and critical thinking. Here are some specific situations in which you can give your kids more autonomy and how it can be beneficial.

1. Choice of Activities: Giving children the freedom to choose their activities can help them develop responsibility and decision-making skills. For example, let your children choose what extracurricular activities they want to participate in, what to do on the weekends, where to go on a field trip, what restaurant to eat at, where to play, what and when to read, and which classes to enroll in.

2. Decisions about Their Appearance: Giving

children the freedom to choose their own clothing and hairstyle is a meaningful way to give them more autonomy and help them develop their sense of identity. It allows them to express themselves in a way that feels authentic to who they are. Allowing your kids to make these choices sends a message that you trust and respect their individuality.

3. Setting Goals: When children are given the autonomy to set their goals, they can develop a greater sense of ownership and motivation. Support your children's academic and personal goals.

4. Learning Pace: Children learn at their own pace, and giving them the autonomy to do so can help them build confidence and independence. Let your children work independently, especially in reading, writing, and math.

5. Problem-Solving: Allowing children to solve problems independently can help them develop critical thinking and problem-solving skills. Encourage your children to come up with solutions to everyday problems.

6. Family Rules: When children are given the autonomy to help set rules, they are more likely to follow them. Involve your kids in creating rules and expectations, which can help promote a sense of responsibility and ownership.

Remember, children are born passionately eager to make as much sense as possible of things around them.

If you attempt to control, manipulate, or divert this process, the independent scientist in the child disappears.

*C*hildren learn from anything and everything they see. They learn wherever they are, not just in special learning places.

—John Holt

HOW TO START

IF YOU HAVE NO CLUE HOW TO START TEACHING your own kids, I have good news! Your role is not to teach at all, but to find opportunities for your children to learn. There are a wealth of resources in the community and the world. Your job is to go look for them. Your job is not to be a teacher but a guide or companion in each process.

Also, if you think you can't educate your children at home because you are not a teacher, please know that teachers don't know how to educate children either until they have been given the standards, a list of what to teach, which they must follow. Each grade has a list of educational standards kids should learn. For example, in kindergarten, they should know to count to 100 and skip counting by five. In first grade, they should know all the sight words. In second grade, they start learning to write book reports and silly stuff like that. You, dear parent, not knowing the standards is fantastic—trust me, fantastic! (If you want to learn each grade level's standards, you can find them online).

Not knowing what your children should be learning if they were in school can actually be an advantage. When you don't have preconceived expectations or artificial timelines for your children's development, you're less likely to judge, pressure, or push your children to learn something they're not ready for. Science and psychology tell us that children develop at their own pace and within a wide range of "normal."

By following your children's lead, you can consider your children's unique strengths and challenges. This approach allows children to learn at their own pace in a natural and comfortable way. When children are free to learn this way, they're less likely to feel pressured, shamed, or remediated if they struggle with certain skills like reading or writing.

When you don't impose the compulsory learning and age-by-age standards onto children, there is space for curiosity, purposefully pursuing learning, and appreciating learning. By allowing children to discover on their own terms, you honor their paths to educational success.

Rather than focusing on what children should be learning at a specific age, take the time to study your own children. Observe them. They are the ones that know what they should be learning, and if you pay attention, your kids will guide you on what to provide so they can learn. Providing is the key. Your kids won't learn if they are in an empty room all day, with no interaction with the environment. Kids must explore, touch, see, hear, and do activities.

Start by living life and working on your relationship with your children. If your kids are infants, then just live your everyday life and bond with them. Children come into the world biologically designed to educate themselves. Their natural curiosity, playfulness, sociability, and playfulness were shaped by natural selection to serve the purpose of their education. So let it happen. Talk, sing, play music, read, and have toys or safe items to play with in every room of the house. Go for a walk and to the grocery store. Anything you do in your everyday life will be great exposure.

If your kids are older when you decide to give them a successful education, start by letting them play. Trust me—play, play, play. Allowing children to play may seem to you as delaying formal academic instruction, but delaying is actually something recommended by educational research. You can wait until your children show signs of being ready. Please resist the urge to compare your children to anyone else's. Everyone is on a different timetable. When you pressure children too soon, a variety of negatives are set in motion.

Play is not frivolous.
It enhances brain structure and function and promotes executive function, which allows chidlren to pursue goals and ignore distractions. Play is fundamentally important for learning twenty-first-century skills, such as problem-solving, collaboration, and creativity, which require the executive functioning skills critical for adult success.

If your kids are teens when you decide to give them a successful education, let them rest, give them free time and let them play. You and your teens need time to de-school your mentality and take a looooong break until they recover. They have to heal from whatever school experiences they had. It takes time for you and them to realize they can learn without the school's typical routines and can always learn wherever they are.

Successful education is about the students leading in the education process and you acting as a facilitator. People practice self-directed education in all the ways you can imagine and probably some you haven't imagined yet. It's difficult to tell you how to do it when I don't even know your children.

You must be open to realizing that learning comes in many different shapes and forms and probably doesn't look anything like what you think "learning" is. Many parents are uncomfortable with this mindset, and you won't get anywhere unless you change your mindset. Children don't have to learn 2 + 2 = 4 in a workbook or paper. They can learn this math fact while playing with cars or dolls in their bedrooms. They can learn to read and write at the beach using a stick or a shell without any book or pen and paper.

Deschool. I'm repeating myself by telling you about deschooling again, but that's how important it is. If you're new to this type of education and went to school as a child, deschooling is a good idea. That means erasing the school mentality from your mind. Many of us have been trained to think in terms of school. The idea is to get you out of the mindset of schooling. We think that learning has to be done a certain way and that any activity that doesn't lead to learning is worthless. That is not true, so take time to get out of that mindset and challenge it.

You must trust that children learn by providing a rich

environment, involving children in everyday living, and helping them find answers to their questions. This is the plan for a successful education. It is that simple.

But how?

This is the hard part because there is no right way to do it, no single way. And parents who are starting want and need to know how to do it. There is no specific answer of what to do because every kid is different. Everyone has different needs, interests, abilities, goals, and environments. What would you say if people told you there was only one way to live your life, one way to do your job? You'd hate it because it would take away your freedom and all the fun.

Telling you how to educate your kids is like taking away your freedom and all the fun out of it. It's really difficult for me to tell you how. I can offer some tips on how you might approach things, but these are just ideas to start you out. You do you.

"There is no difference between living and learning… it is impossible and misleading and harmful to think of them as being separate."—John Holt

Your kids will question everything, and finding the answers makes their education successful because the learning will be meaningful. When your kids ask a question, that's an opportunity to discover something. Look it up together. Look for books in the library or a documentary. Just yesterday, my daughter asked me why ice floats and rocks sink while I was driving the car. I learned that in school but couldn't explain it to her. When we got home, we searched the internet for an explanation and learned all about density.

People you know—friends, family, neighbors, and other parents who educate at home—might be fantastic teachers. A family member of mine is a firefighter. He loved it when I asked him to do a workshop for my kids. He did a terrific job educating them, and my kids learned important fire lessons. Do you know a journalist? An actor? A mechanic? A dentist? A lawyer? They would love to help you educate your kids. Even the business you often visit (coffee shop, restaurant, or dry cleaning) would like to help you.

Games are great resources. Play all kinds of games. Outdoor games, board games, cards, and age-appropriate video games are fantastic for learning the basics of reading, writing, math, and other subjects. My kids learned all about taxes while playing Monopoly, and my youngest mastered his basic math skills by playing Mario.

Try to say *yes* more. If your kids want to do messy art projects, say *yes*. Say *yes* if your kids want to bake cookies and you just finished cleaning the kitchen. If they want to play outdoors when it is raining, say *yes*. Say *yes* if they want to camp the camping tent in the living room for a week. Say *yes* if they want to leave the toys in the living room because they'll play with them again tomorrow.

Expose them to everything possible. Get out and explore your town, ride your bikes, go to different parks, meet different people, lay books and magazines around the house, watch shows about interesting things, go see a musical or a sporting event, go on a trip, get exposure to everything. This will help your children explore new interests. Even if they don't seem interested at first, the exposure will allow them to find new things on their own. Show them the world and the value of experiences over things. Explore with your children, get outdoors, and learn about the world around you. Curiosity will always open doors and lead down new, exciting paths full of adventure and learning.

Observe them. Figuring out what works for your kids is what makes their education successful. Try different things, observe your kids, and eventually, your kids will carve the path. Follow it.

Give them free, unstructured time. You don't have to entertain or keep your kids busy all the time. Having boring time, free time, and unstructured time is also crucial. Unstructured play is a great way to nurture and develop your children's curiosity and sense of discovery. By allowing your children to be curious and explore, you help them develop confidence and appreciation.

Pursue their interests. If it's a silly or one-day interest, follow it. It will lead to more learning.

Be patient and trust. You will see the results later. Progress in your children will happen over time. Trust is important. It's hard in the beginning, but it's important to trust that kids can learn on their own with minimal guidance. They will learn if they're interested in something or need something.

Give them a rich environment. A space in which children can learn easily and naturally all the time is important. Provide an environment designed to support and promote a wide range of learning experiences and opportunities for kids. Equip it with diverse resources, such as books, technology, manipulatives, art supplies, nature, and games and hands-on learning opportunities that allow them to explore, experiment, and problem-solve. Give opportunities for kids to work collaboratively, communicate with their peers, and develop important social and interpersonal skills. Be welcoming, inclusive, and supportive to encourage kids to take risks, make mistakes, and learn from them. Create an environment that is tailored to the needs and interests of each kid. The environment is your home, the woods, or any spot with nature—the park and the community.

When children are very young, it's practical to remove the items that you don't want them to touch or break (fancy books on the coffee table, decorations on shelves, and dangerous cleaning supplies) and replace them with items that can be touched (toys, children's books, pots, and pans). That way, your kids can freely explore, learning constantly, without interrupting their curiosity with the typical sentence adults constantly say, "Don't touch this!"

The more freedom little ones have to explore and the less "No" and "Don't play with this" they hear, the better. Try to say *no* only when it's critical. Save the word *no* for dangerous situations like "No, don't touch the hot fireplace" or "No, don't cross the street."

A rich environment doesn't mean purchasing fancy expensive toys. It means having interesting things around to observe and explore. Kids happily play with a second-hand kitchen that a neighbor placed on the street for somebody to grab. Kids love playing with cheap items like straws; clean, recycled pantry items; and old pots and pans. Kids enjoy playing with old clothes you don't wear anymore and crave playing outside in the woods.

A rich environment means providing opportunities and activities. Talk to your kids, play music, place toys where they're easy to grab, and take your children places. Step back, and give them space to explore and play.

The trick to giving children a successful education is to let them learn how to learn and teach themselves. If kids know how to learn and teach themselves, they'll be prepared for the future. If the things your children know become obsolete in the future, then the person who knows how to learn anything will be ready to learn whatever is in use and succeed.

"But what does a day look like?"

It's hard to tell you what a normal day looks like, because every unschooling environment is different. I can tell you that it looks like a Saturday, or your day off, or perhaps summertime. What do you do on your day off? I think educating our kids freely looks like your day off.

Some families go to museums and children's parks or for a hike or a swim. Some families relax at home, letting their kids play in their backyard and maybe with neighbors or arrange playdates, later watching a cozy movie on the sofa. Other families go on short trips, play sports, or enjoy a sports event. There is a structure if that's what you and your family need, or there's no structure if you and your family need freedom.

When my kids were younger, some days were spent at home playing all day. They played so much while I read John Holt's books, one by one, cuddled in my living room. Other days were spent cleaning the house, cooking in the kitchen, reading—so much reading, and watching a movie. Some days we were never home. We would pack lunch and lots of snacks and spend the day in the woods, lake, or river with some friends. And some days looked more academic. We would go to the library to get new books, spend time reading children's magazines, attending a class or a workshop, and attend the classes the homeschool coop organized.

"But if we only play and live like every day is a Saturday, how will they learn the basics?"

All the evidence of childhood development supports that children are inherently motivated. Reading, writing, and arithmetic are basic life skills. Children pick them up as byproducts of living in an interesting, stimulating, and text-rich environment. Their learning is seamlessly integrated with their lives; rather than studying the basics as discrete objects during discrete periods, they absorb them as ways of thinking while they pursue other interests and goals. The basics are so important to functioning independently in our world that children eventually have a very good reason to acquire them and, motivated by that reason, do so rapidly.

Children who are free to self-direct their education

learn just like adults: based on what interests them, figuring out how to learn it on their own, changing as they change, using whatever resources and learning materials they find, driven by curiosity and practical application rather than because someone says it's important. This way of learning is how I learned to cook, decorate my house, drive, fix a door knob and my dryer, be a good kindergarten teacher, parent, advocate for unschooling, self-published a book, and market my book. It's how our children will learn when they're adults. Why not have them learn like that now?

"But how do we know they are learning?"

If you get to know your children—watch them, listen to them, spend time talking with them, sit with them, and be with them—you'll collect all the data necessary to prove your children are learning. Trust me.

Here's an example. I knew my kids were learning to write because I saw it in their games. They wrote the menu and prices on paper when they played pretend store or restaurant. Also, every year around Christmas time, they wrote a list of the items they wanted to get for presents. Every year I got to witness their writing improving. When they got older and enrolled in classes, the homework in those classes required writing, and that's when I saw they could write well.

You will know your kids are learning. Trust me. Oh, let me tell you, my kids were like walking encyclopedias! My daughter used to go on and on about dog breeds—their quirks, where they're from, you name it. And my son? He was a geography wiz. He would tell me all about different countries—their populations, famous landmarks, and capitals. As for my oldest, he had a real knack for explaining all sorts of things—current events, political drama, history, and science facts. I swear, listening to them talk was enough to wear me out!

"But how can we support our children's passions and interests if we don't know what they are?"

There are several signs that your child may be passionate about a particular activity or interest. Here are a few of them.

- Enthusiasm: Your children's genuine excitement and eagerness towards a particular activity or interest may indicate a passion for it.
- Curiosity: If your children frequently ask questions or actively seek information about a specific activity or interest, it may indicate that they have a passion for it.
- Natural Ability: If your children have a natural talent or aptitude for a specific activity or interest, it may indicate that they have a passion for it.
- Creativity: If your children enjoy exploring various ways of doing things or experimenting with different approaches to a specific activity or interest, it can signify a passion for it.
- Dedication: If your children remain committed to practicing or improving in a specific activity

or interest, even when faced with difficulties or requires significant time and effort, it can be a sign that they have a passion for it.

• Joy and Fulfillment: If your children experience joy and fulfillment from a specific activity or interest, giving them a sense of purpose or meaning can signify a passion for it.

Some interests will last a day, and some will last for years. Some passions may be expensive, and you may cringe when your children quit and drop that interest. However, it's important to remember that your money did not go in vain. Your children learned, and you invested in their growth and development.

It's important to understand that every child is unique and will discover interests at their own pace. When children don't have particular passions or interests, encourage them to explore different options and find what they enjoy by allowing them to try new things and experiment with different activities. Encourage them to explore a variety of activities and be open to trying new things by enrolling in art classes, music lessons, sports teams, volunteering, joining clubs, doing an activity you have never ever done, changing your daily routine, or surprising them with a new book, magazine, recipe, documentary, or anything else. Do not force your children into a particular activity or interest; allow them to quit if they are not enjoying it. It's important to remember that every child is unique, and passions and interests develop at different stages.

Meanwhile, live your life. Let your children marvel at

everything. What starts as a small curiosity can lead to a future profession.

"How do I know I'm doing a good job?"

You will know you are doing well by observing your children's happiness and motivation to learn.

If your children are happy, you are doing a great job. This does not mean that you have to please your children 24/7 or that your children can never cry. Crying and sad moments are part of life. What I mean is that your children should be happy overall.

Suppose your children are motivated to learn anything, regardless of the subject, and are engaged, passionate, interested, and curious. In that case, you know you are doing a good job. If your children's motivation disappears, they are no longer interested in learning anything. Nothing seems to matter. Pay attention because something is wrong.

If you sometimes feel like you need to do more or a better job, offer your children various opportunities. For example, you can suggest activities such as visiting the zoo, getting a new book, enrolling in a class, or going on a field trip. It's important to be okay with your children's answer and respect their choices, because they drive their education.

You'll do great if you observe, provide, and respect.

Learning is not the product of teaching. Learning is the product of the activity of learners.

—John Holt

SPECIAL NEEDS, THE GIFTED CHILD, AND THE RELUCTANT LEARNER

THE PERFECT EDUCATION FOR YOUR CHILD doesn't exist. You have to create it.

Now and then, a parent asks me what homeschool curriculum or method works best for children diagnosed with an autism spectrum disorder. I wish it would be as easy as going online and purchasing the perfect education with a click of a button.

The perfect education for all children—diagnosed or not, learning disabilities or not, gifted or not—is the one you create by observing and providing what they need. Unschooling works well for every child regardless of the diagnosis because self-directed education is the perfect, curated, personalized, and tailored IEP.

Many families in the U.S. choose to educate at home because their children have special needs. And many families from other countries where home education is unheard of asked me if homeschooling would be a good idea for children with certain learning difficulties. Yes! Absolutely! You don't need to be a special education expert to be an expert on your children.

An IEP, or individualized education plan, is a document created by a team of school employees that is legally binding for teachers and staff. It means they must teach and treat your children the way their team has deemed best. Successful education is already an IEP, and you are in charge of creating the team. Being taught at home is automatically an individualized experience. As such, it's the best there is.

Educating at home or a self-directed education center is great for children with mental blocks that don't allow them to learn in the traditional school setting. In fact, some difficulties actually disappear when children are home, feeling safe and happy, away from the pressure of school that makes them feel less.

Some of your learners' struggles will disappear when you change the environment, remove the pressure, and change the educational method. Once children feel safe and comfortable, they start to shine and learn. Many challenges disappear when you personalize a learning program because you are not forcing a unique child to go through the typical, standard program many conventional schools use.

Your kids need all the loving attention, support, and encouragement they can get. Educating at home can become a sanity-saving for some children. Your children can blossom when you are in charge of setting the schedule, curriculum, and pace. Whatever works for you and your kids goes. You don't need permission from anyone to customize your kids' learning.

As usual, follow their passions. This method lets you start with their strengths and use them to engage.

Knowledge is power. Search, study, and learn all you can about your kids' specific challenges. Find other parents homeschooling special-needs children and learn from them, read some books, and follow some experts on social media. Take a class or two about your children's label and study, search, and learn all about your children's particular diagnoses. Stay informed, as there is absolutely no need for you to figure it all out yourself. There is a wealth of resources online to help you learn everything you need to know to be successful. Usually, parents become experts on their kids' disabilities and they become great educators. You will too.

When teachers gets their degrees in special education, they spend years studying how to educate children with a wide range of disabilities. You, however, only need to focus on the specific disability (or disabilities) present in your family.

Please note that many kids are misdiagnosed with learning disabilities when, in fact, they are experiencing trauma. Kids with traumatic memories have problems focusing attention and learning new information. It is important to get the correct diagnosis to treat it accurately.

Laws concerning homeschooling special-needs

children vary in each state. Find out the legal requirements and rules to educate at home special-needs children in your area. Usually, homeschool groups in your area have a lot of info, as at least one family usually has a child with some kind of special need. And search the Department of Developmental Disabilities website of your state or country. Your pediatrician's office, local school district website, state's behavioral healthcare services website, and hslda.org have helpful information too.

Rest assured that if your gut is pulling you to educate your kids at home, it's because it's the perfect way to put success in your kids' hands. Here's why:

- Your children are the focus of the education process. You get to tailor it perfectly for them.
- You get to adapt everything you do.
- You can individualize instruction to your children's needs.
- You will witness the magical moment of your kids mastering something they struggled with.
- Your children have the opportunity to learn at their own pace.
- You can choose an educational style or method that works for your kid.
- Your children have the freedom to learn new skills when they are ready.
- It helps develop self-confidence.
- And it gives your learner a personalized education that engages and inspires them.

Make sure you have a support team. It's important to take care of yourself. Educating a special-needs child is a demanding and stressful task at times. Parents work hard and worry so much that they eventually experience burnout from fatigue, illness, anxiety, stress, etc. Don't let this happen to you. Ask for help or find resources to help you take breaks.

Don't try to do it all by yourself. Think about it this way—parents often hire a music tutor because they don't know how to teach their children to play the violin or piano. You can hire a professional to help you with whatever you are not an expert on.

You might be eligible for free resources. Different states have different rules and regulations about how children who have disabilities can receive services from school districts. Some school districts are legally responsible for identifying and evaluating children with special needs. Once evaluated, many states will provide services to your children.

Educating at home is full of challenges, and while you can fully educate your children, there will be times when you need help. For example, your children may need therapy, or you may need extra help from a tutor. Getting help from professionals does not lessen the work you are doing day in and day out.

There are support groups for parents who are homeschooling special-needs children. State homeschooling organizations, special-needs organizations, and groups like the National Challenged Homeschoolers Associated Network provide support and a wealth of resources.

Take things one step at a time, seek help when needed, and trust yourself. You can do it!

Even though public schools have resources that you most likely do not have at home, many parents transition from public school to homeschooling and find great success.

Additional resources include:
- understood.org
- nathhan.com
- tacanow.org
- gemmlearning.com
- wilostar3d.com

The gifted child and the twice exceptional learner

Our society has established a normative path for all of us to follow. However, when raising and educating gifted children or gifted children with learning disabilities, traditional education offered by schools and homeschool curriculums do not meet their needs. Self-directed education is a form of education that benefits all children—ALL. Parenting and educating these amazing children requires a distinct approach that differs from most conventional parenting styles.

When you have children who think in highly accelerated, divergent ways that are out-of-the-box, traditional brick-and-mortar schooling is not only a poor fit but is also potentially damaging and regressive.

If you have gifted children, it is essential to take the time to deschool. Shifting your mindset away from schooling and toward a learning mindset will benefit you and your children. The best gift you can give your children is to allow them to take control of their education. By doing so, you will discover that the things that your kids are interested in learning about are more valuable and worthwhile than what is typically taught in schools. Let them learn on their own terms. They are wired that way. We all are.

The more divergent and asynchronous gifted children are, the less likely any prescribed curriculum or schooling approach will work. These children question everything. They yearn to know more and ask questions that don't easily have answers. This passionate curiosity is best supported when no limits restrict open-ended learning.

Creative intellectuals cannot be restricted. Your children's minds need to delve deeply into their areas of interest. If you want your children to be successful, give them as much autonomy as possible, especially in their learning. They are great at finding their interests and delving deeply into subject areas that they find appealing.

Honor your children's individual needs and allow them to flourish without anyone's agenda interfering. Be a facilitator, offering support and guidance. You'll see your kids demonstrate interest and motivation in learning, and you'll see them engaged and participating in discussions and activities. You won't be teaching them. They'll teach you.

Trust your learner.

A couple other resources to consider are:
• sengifted.org
• nagc.org

The reluctant learner

Many books and articles written by professionals tell you the best ways to engage reluctant learners are:

- Involve them in the decision-making process. For instance, ask them to weigh in. When learners know their contribution matters, they are more likely to engage in the educational process.

- Focus on what your kids do well. Focusing on what children do well does more than foster good feelings; it also equips them to succeed in the future.

- Get to know and connect with your kids. Uncover their passions and find out their interests. Such connections honor your kids' values and can increase their sense of belonging.

- Relate lessons to learners' interests. Your education plan will come to life if it offers real-world applications. The more children can relate what they're learning to what they care about, the more they are likely to engage in learning.

- Present new concepts in bite-size pieces. Rather than delivering a full lecture on a new topic, focus on presenting chunks of new information with short, interactive activities. This allows your kids to speak up about difficulties as they arise rather than waiting until those challenges feel insurmountable.

- Be there to support your kids. This is the most obvious—and the most difficult—way to engage reluctant learners: Let them know they can access help whenever and wherever they need it.

As you can see, these effective strategies for engaging reluctant learners are the same as unschooling! Allowing children to self-direct their learning and being supportive will make the resistance disappear. The more reluctant children are to learn, the more autonomy they need in selecting what they learn.

Empower your children's learning journey! Reluctant learners won't be resistant when they have control over their learning. Liberate your learners, let them take the lead, and watch them thrive.

*P*eople do not always learn from experience,
but without it they do not learn at all.

—John Holt

THE BENEFITS OF
A PART-TIME JOB

AS YOUR TEENAGERS GROW OLDER AND TAKE
on more responsibilities, help them to obtain their first
job once they reach the age of 15 or 16 so they can start
earning their own money while pursuing their interests,
passions, and dream careers. Help them find good, safe
jobs that fit well with their schedule. It will teach them
responsibility, give them some new freedom, and give
them peace of mind for you and them knowing they will
have an income while pursuing their dreams.

By earning money, they will feel more independent
and empowered. Working part-time is a great way for
your children to transition into making their own money
and learning to manage it effectively. They will learn important lessons in money management, from earning to
spending to saving. They will have a greater appreciation
for money because they understand the effort and time
it took to earn it.

Working during adolescence can help develop essential skills such as time management, organization, communication, and teamwork. Additionally, it can establish

a work history that can be valuable in their future professional endeavors. While most job descriptions have specific technical requirements, numerous soft skills set individuals apart, including conflict resolution, effective communication, problem-solving, and social skills for customer service.

Working can help build character by teaching teenagers responsibility and accountability. It can also provide opportunities for them to learn how to take initiative, function independently, and fulfill commitments.

In addition, working enables teenagers to establish connections with adult employers who may serve as future references. As your children work part-time, they become aware of their capabilities, which builds their confidence and self-reliance. This newfound sense of independence and responsibility can encourage them to further their development with confidence.

My son's initial job was at a local coffee shop, where he remains employed to this day. He has steadily increased his salary as he advances in the company and pursues his writing. With his earnings, he could purchase a car, travel abroad, and cover his expenses while establishing his writing career.

My daughter's first job is at the local grocery store. She earned significant money to spend on concert tickets and Cirque du Soleil shows and gained valuable social experience. She works alongside other teenagers—some are homeschooled, and others attend a traditional school. They all enjoy their time together. She calls her job her high school experience.

She makes a considerable sum of money, which gives me peace of mind because if I couldn't pay for the plane ticket for her upcoming audition in Europe, she could cover the cost herself.

And my younger son will start his first job as a lifeguard this summer after completing his training. He is eager to invest his earnings.

Oh! And working can count as a high school credit. Add "Work Ethics 1 Credit" to your child's high school transcript.

*I*t is as true now as it was then that no matter what tests show, very little of what is taught in school is learned, very little of what is learned is remembered, and very little of what is remembered is used. The things we learn, remember, and use are the things we seek out or meet in the daily, serious, nonschool parts of our lives.

—John Holt

HIGH SCHOOL TRANSCRIPT

A SUCCESSFUL EDUCATION LOOKS VERY different from the education you experienced or what society tells us a high school education is supposed to look like. You allowed your teens the freedom to learn about what interests them in the way that makes the most sense.

Since giving autonomy to your kids' education means you have not followed the academic standards that traditional schools do, writing a transcript seems daunting. I know, I was petrified too, but it turns out it is easy. This is your chance to use your creative skills and name everything your kid has done into a course. Go online and search for high school transcripts to familiarize yourself with the wording and the format. Observe what they look like, what words they use, and what kind of format is common. Get familiar with high school credits and electives. An easy way to do this is to search private schools' websites or online schools and pay attention to their academics (classes, courses, and electives).

Creating a high school transcript has different

approaches. It depends on where your children are heading. Suppose you know for certain your children are heading to college. In that case, you and your children need to talk about what knowledge or classes are important to have in that transcript to be accepted to college. It's time to focus on getting credits from classes or apprenticeships to help you follow the college path.

If you are sure your children are not going to college, you will create a transcript focusing on the future job your children are trying to get. For example, if one of your children wants to work in a daycare center, it would look great in the transcript if your child took some child development classes, got CPR certified, and volunteered in a preschool. Or, if your child is planning on working in a dog hotel business, it would look great if the transcript had some dog psychology classes, dog training courses, and volunteer hours at a dog shelter.

And if your child is becoming an entrepreneur, there is no need for a high school transcript.

If you are still determining your teens' path, let them continue self-directing their education. This is when self-directed adolescents take the reins and start taking classes or other learning routes to pursue their dreams. When it's time to create the transcript, if your kids haven't done enough to create a full transcript, ask them to take the classes or study in their own way the subjects they are missing for their transcript to look official.

Many parents create their kids' transcripts from scratch, and colleges accept them. You can too. It's easy, so don't be intimidated. You can do it, and it can be done for free. There are templates online that you can copy, but if you are afraid of creating your kid's transcript on your own, know that you can use an umbrella school or a transcript service like hsdla.org

Main components of the high school transcript include:

- The student's name, date of birth, homeschool name, address, phone number, and social security number (it's up to you)
- Graduation date
- A section for each grade or subject area in which high school courses were completed, with the grades earned for each course and the credits given for each course
- The number of credits (both cumulative and, if organized by year, for each year)
- GPA (cumulative and, if organized by year, for each year)
- Grading scale
- Your signature

You can find a free GPA high school calculator online. Generally, a full-year high school course is worth one credit, and a semester course is half a credit. Every state has different requirements, but after your online search, you'll notice the pattern is more or less like this:

- 4 credits of English, including literature and writing
- 3–4 credits of math, including a minimum of Algebra I, Algebra II, Geometry, and Trigonometry

- 2–4 credits of social sciences, such as World History, World Geography, U.S. History, and U.S. Government
- 2–3 credits of lab sciences, such as Biology, Chemistry, and Physics
- 2+ credits of the same foreign language
- 6 electives for the balance (electives can be anything, including driver's ed, volunteering, and work)

You can put together a transcript using your creative thinking, trying to match what your students have learned in unconventional ways into the traditional naming. For example, my son read an astrophysics book and never took a class or an exam. Still, he learned, so we wrote on his transcript 'Introduction to Astrophysics.' My daughter learned Egyptian history by watching a series of well-done YouTube documentaries. She didn't attend any history class, but she did learn, so we added "Egyptian History' to her transcript.

Find out how many credits your students need to graduate. You may need to follow your state guidance, or you may need to follow the admission rules of the college your kids want to attend. Keep an open dialogue with your teens. Bring them into the transcript writing process and give them ownership over it. You can be there to guide them.

You do not need your transcript to be accredited by anyone; it only needs to be notarized if a college specifically requests it. At the moment of writing this book, no state in the U.S.A. requires a home education program to be accredited. Most colleges, universities, and trade schools don't require it either. You don't even need accreditation to be accepted to an Ivy League school! But stay informed, because rules change. As of right now, more and more colleges are joining the movement of not asking for the SAT and ACT test results.

Most colleges have information on their websites about admission for homeschooled students. It may be surprising to many people to find out that unschoolers and self-directed learners are being sought-after by colleges and universities.

Course descriptions are not part of a homeschool transcript. Course descriptions are completely separate documents and often aren't required at all. Your teens' high school transcripts are snapshots of what they did in high school and how hard they worked during those four years.

"What about the diploma?"

A diploma is a certificate of completion. You can make one if you want. It does not get sent to colleges. It is a symbol showing that your kids fulfilled the graduation requirements. You can make one using templates online. It is much easier to create than the transcript.

Remember, if your teens are possibly college bound, learning about colleges and universities is a great way to know how to approach the high school years. However, if your teens do not plan on attending college, let them learn freely and have fun creating their special high school transcript, which they might not even need to show anyone. My son, for example, is now twenty years old, has become a writer, and hasn't had to show his transcript to any publishing company.

And finally, another approach to creating a high school transcript is to create a draft of what your teens' transcripts are supposed to look like. They can use that as a guide or checklist. This way, your learners can choose when, how, and what to learn.

The following pages provide samples of transcripts to help you get started.

Official High School Transcript

Student: Markos Rios
Year 2021-2024
Academy: Rios Unschooling
1 Main Street, Miami, FL
Instructor: Mia Rios

GRADE 9TH

SUBJECT	GRADE	CREDIT
MATH	B	2
ENGLISH	B	2
HISTORY	A	2
SCIENCE	A	2
ELECTIVE I	A	2
ELECTIVE II	A	2
PHYSICAL EDUCATION	A	2

GPA TOTAL 4.3

GRADE 10TH

SUBJECT	GRADE	CREDIT
MATH	B	2
ENGLISH	B	2
HISTORY	A	2
SCIENCE	A	2
ELECTIVE I	A	2
ELECTIVE II	A	2
PHYSICAL EDUCATION	A	2

GPA TOTAL 4.3

GRADE 11TH

SUBJECT	GRADE	CREDIT
MATH	B	2
ENGLISH	B	2
HISTORY	A	2
SCIENCE	A	2
ELECTIVE I	A	2
ELECTIVE II	A	2
PHYSICAL EDUCATION	A	2

GPA TOTAL 4.3

GRADE 12TH

SUBJECT	GRADE	CREDIT
MATH	B	2
ENGLISH	B	2
HISTORY	A	2
SCIENCE	A	2
ELECTIVE I	A	2
ELECTIVE II	A	2
PHYSICAL EDUCATION	A	2

GPA TOTAL 4.3
GPA 4 YEARS TOTAL 4.1
CREDIT TOTALS:

SIGNATURE AUTHORIZATION

HIGH SCHOOL TRANSCRIPT
(Grades 9-12)

Graduation Date: 05/30/2013

School of Record
Sample School Name
Sample Parent
1234 Town Road
Anywhere, VA 22345
123-456-7890
info@fasttranscripts.com

Student Information
Sample Student
Gender: M
Date of Birth: 12/08/1995
1234 Town Road
Anywhere, VA 22345
123-456-7890
info@fasttranscripts.com

Course Study - Grade 9	Grade	Credits
Lit / Composition	A	1
Algebra 1	A	1
Physical Science	B	1
Geography	B	1
Spanish 1	C	1
Physical Ed	PASS	.5
Health	B	.5
Instrumental Music	A	.5
GPA = 3.25		6.5

Course Study - Grade 10	Grade	Credits
World Literature	A	1
Geometry	B	1
Biology / Lab	B	1
World History	A	1
Spanish 2	B	1
Physical Ed	PASS	.5
Choir	A	.5
GPA = 3.45		6

Course Study - Grade 11	Grade	Credits
American Literature	A	1
Algebra 2	A	1
United States History	A	1
Chemistry / Lab	B	1
Spanish 101*	B	1
Computer Applications	A	.5
Logic	B	1
GPA = 3.54		6.5

Course Study - Grade 12	Grade	Credits
AP: English Language	B	1
Pre-Calculus	B	1
Physics	A	1
United States Government	A	.5
Economics	A	.5
Debate	B	1
Financial Management	A	1
GPA = 3.67		6

Summary By Grade				
Grade	9th	10th	11th	12th
Cum. GPA	3.25	3.35	3.42	3.48
Credits Earned	6.5	6	6.5	6

Cumulative Summary (9th - 12th)			
Total Credits	GPA Credits	GPA Points	GPA
25.00	24.00	83.50	3.48

Grading Scale				
90 - 100	80 - 89	70 - 79	60 - 69	0 - 59
A	B	C	D	F

Commentary
*ACE Community College

Authorized Signature   Date: 01/27/2014

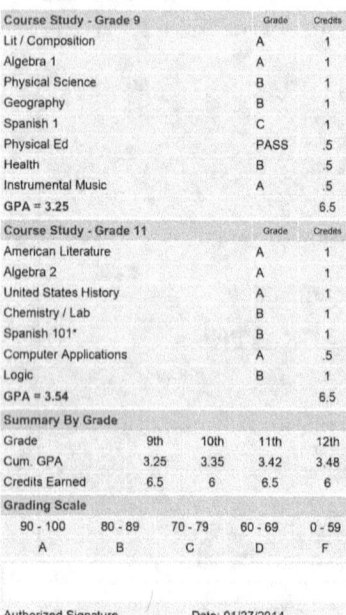

SMITH ACADEMY
OFFICIAL HIGH SCHOOL TRANSCRIPT

STUDENT INFORMATION	SCHOOL INFORMATION
FULL NAME: First Middle Last	**NAME:** Homeschool Name
ADDRESS: 123 Main Street	**ADDRESS:** 123 Main Street
Cityname, St 56879	Cityname, St 56879
PHONE NUMBER: 111-555-1234	**PHONE NUMBER:** 111-555-1234
EMAIL ADDRESS: emailname@email.com	**EMAIL ADDRESS:** homeschoolname@email.com
DATE OF BIRTH: 02/17/93	
PARENT/GUARDIAN: Father and Mother Lastname	

ACADEMIC RECORD

SCHOOL YEAR: 2006-2007 GRADE LEVEL: 9th			SCHOOL YEAR: 2007-2008 GRADE LEVEL: 10th		
Course Title	Credit Earned	Final Grade	Course Title	Credit Earned	Final Grade
English 9	1.0	A	English 10	1.0	B
Algebra I	1.0	A	Geometry	1.0	B
Biology w/lab	1.0	B	Chemistry w/lab	1.0	C
Geography	1.0	C	World History	1.0	A
Latin I	1.0	A	Latin II	1.0	B
Logic	1.0	B	Rhetoric	1.0	A
Fine Arts: Piano	0.5	B	Fine Arts: Piano II	0.5	B
Theology	0.5	A	Old Testament Survey	0.5	B
Total Credits: 7.0 **GPA:** 3.36 **Cumulative GPA:** 3.36			**Total Credits:** 7.0 **GPA:** 3.14 **Cumulative GPA:** 3.25		

SCHOOL YEAR: 2008-2009 GRADE LEVEL: 11th			SCHOOL YEAR: 2009-2010 GRADE LEVEL: 12th		
Course Title	Credit Earned	Final Grade	Course Title	Credit Earned	Final Grade
English 11	1.0	A	English 12	1.0	A
Algebra II	1.0	A	Trigonometry/Pre-Calculus	1.0	A
Physics	1.0	B	US Government	1.0	A
US History	1.0	A	Economics *	1.0	B
Spanish I	1.0	B	Speech *	1.0	A
Philosophy	1.0	B	Spanish II	1.0	C
Fine Arts: Piano III	0.5	B	Fine Arts: Drawing	0.5	B
New Testament Survey	0.5	A	Apologetics	0.5	B
Total Credits: 7.0 **GPA:** 3.57 **Cumulative GPA:** 3.36			**Total Credits:** 7.0 **GPA:** 3.43 **Cumulative GPA:** 3.38		

ACADEMIC SUMMARY	GRADING SCALE	NOTES
Cumulative GPA: 3.38	90 – 100 = A	* Coursework taken at a local community college. Official
Credits Earned: 28.0	80 – 89 = B	transcript from college has been requested and will be sent to
	70 – 79 = C	you shortly. *(add any applicable notes here)*
Diploma Earned: yes	60 – 69 = D	
Graduation Date: 6/30/2010	59 – below = F	

I do hereby self-certify and affirm that this is the official transcript and record of Jane B. Smith in the academic studies of 2006 – 2010.

Signature: Title: Principal   Date: June 30, 2010

To trust children we must first learn to trust ourselves . . . and most of us were taught as children that we could not be trusted.

—John Holt

HOW TO CONVINCE YOUR PARTNER?

MANY FAMILIES DO NOT EXPERIENCE THE
privilege of giving their children a successful education
because one spouse can't persuade the other to follow that
route. And many moms have asked me for help in this
matter. But it's not always the case that the mom wants to
educate at home or at a radical alternative school, while
the dad is against it. I have a friend whose husband was
the one that convinced her to unschool.

Many spouses or significant others do not want to
educate in an alternative way because they do not have
information about this kind of life. Lack of knowledge
equals fear, misinterpretation, and dismissal. Your job
is to gather all the information necessary to prove that
self-directed education is the right path for your kids.
But it is only fair that your partner does the same to convince you, because school is not the default option. Ask
your partner to gather information proving that school is
the best educational method.

Discuss the fact that alternative educational methods

are legitimate options, not inferior ones. Choosing to educate without the traditional school doesn't mean your children are dumb, you are weirdos, or you are rebels. It means that you want the best for your children. And cookie-cutter education is not the best.

What is your partner afraid of? Ask them to pinpoint every doubt and fear, and you can slowly break them down, educating them. There are books (oh, so many books!), articles, magazines, videos, and social media influencers that will help your partner realize that autonomy in education is the best way.

Arm yourself with a lot of information about educating successfully, whether in unschooling or democratic schools. Try to look at it from your partner's perspective. They are concerned about their children's education and want to ensure it's quality. Act slowly and steadily, and don't overwhelm them. If they feel understood and see that you are listening and willing to properly address their concerns, they are much more likely to relax and give you the green light. Showing your partner examples of other families who educated their kids without school will teach them this kind of education is successful. Try it so they can see results. Once people see natural learning in action, they're converted.

Your partner may think education without school is not conventional enough and fear it would hurt your kids' future prospects. There are some common misunderstandings about self-directed education that you should clear up.

Your partner may think unschooling isn't actually

education. This misconception implies that unschooling is a form of neglect or lack of education. Still, unschooling is a valid and valuable approach to education that prioritizes child-led learning and personalized educational experiences.

One thing your spouse might be worried about is your kids not being able to make friends. Your partner assumes you'll lock your kids in the house, limiting their chance to make friends. While self-directed education provides an individualized approach to education, it does not necessarily lead to isolation. In fact, many unschooling families participate in co-ops, meetups, and community activities to provide ample opportunities for their children to socialize. Some parents fear that not attending school will isolate their children, forgetting that children can make friends after school hours during vacations, at the library, at the park, in extracurricular classes, in church, or in a community center—everywhere.

Another thing your spouse might be worried about is that you need to be more knowledgeable to teach physics, math, or science. Explain to your partner that your children don't have to learn difficult subjects from you. There are plenty of opportunities to learn from people, books, courses, and videos. Children don't have to learn it all from Mom and Dad. Some parents with only a high school diploma are facilitating their children's education at home and doing a very good job of it.

Your partner may be scared of too much freedom and lack of structure, but that's not entirely true. While there may be less structure than in traditional schooling, unschooling involves intentional learning experiences and guidance from parents or other mentors. It's not a completely unregulated approach to education but a more flexible and personalized approach that allows for exploration and curiosity.

Then there is the common fear that unconventional education, like unschooling, may hinder children's future opportunities, such as attending college or finding jobs. Many unschooled children pursue higher education, establish businesses, and succeed in various careers. The personalized learning experiences, when children lead their learning, equip children with the skills needed for success in a range of fields.

Reassure your partner that unschooling is not an excuse for lazy parenting. It is a type of parenting that nurtures children's innate drive to play, explore, and socialize. Honoring children's autonomy, preserving their self-concept, and supporting their interests and ideas requires hard work.

Here are some inspiring TedTalks to encourage your partner

- "Schools Kill Creativity: What Can We Do About It?" by Prince Ea
- "The Future of Learning" by Sugata Mitra
- "How to Develop Your Creative Confidence" by David Kelley
- "How School Makes Kids Less Intelligent" by Eddy Zhong

- "Homeschooling for My Son" by Shantanu Gupta
- "Unschooling" by Alice Khimasia
- "School Is Optional" by Ken Danford
- "Learning through Unschooling" by Callie Vandewiele
- "The Surprising Truth about Learning in Schools" by Will Richardson
- "Self-Learning" by Ryan Lee

*L*iving is learning and when kids are living fully and energetically and happily they are learning a lot, even if we don't always know what it is.

—John Holt

A STRICT STATE

EDUCATING WITHOUT SCHOOL IS ALLOWED IN the United States and many other countries as long as the children are somehow educated. Some countries require rigorous annual assessments to protect children's learning rights. Some states in the U.S. give you a variety of options for you to choose how to assess your children. In some states, you don't have to show anybody your education plan or your kids' progress. Make sure you find out your state regulations.

When you embrace self-directed education and your children's learning is meaningful, there is no need to evaluate them to ensure they are learning. Unfortunately, some school officials don't understand that the best person to evaluate a student's progress is the student. True free learners know when they understand a subject or a skill and when they do not.

Many families choose to not assess their children using standardized tests because the whole purpose of educating differently than the school is that our kids don't get a standard education. Instead, these families write assessments, stating that their children have progressed adequately in all required subjects. Many states allow you to write a report and show a portfolio instead of testing.

You know—or you have learned by reading this book—that allowing children to learn and explore on their own terms is essential. However, some states and countries have a lot of rules for families who educate without school, making it difficult to give children freedom. While it is a right to choose how to educate your children, some states and some countries require proof that you are educating them and not neglecting them. Families living in a strict country or state with harsh laws still have options to educate their children following their pace and interests.

Some families choose to enroll their children in a democratic school, where their kids can play all day long while learning what interests them the most. These schools are a fantastic place for children to grow up.

Some families prefer the additional support offered by umbrella schools. Enrollment in an umbrella school typically satisfies the state's and country's compulsory attendance law, meaning that the family does not need to submit a homeschool form to their education department. These families prefer interacting with an umbrella school rather than social workers or school districts. These schools do not exist to provide instruction. They exist to provide legal cover for home education. They help with paperwork and recordkeeping, and you and your children can choose how and what to learn.

Some families follow a humble and simple, free or very cheap homeschool curriculum to please the state regulations. However, they are not following it rigidly.

They are flexible, use it as a guide, and fully respect their children's pace.

And some families meet the requirements of their state's home education law while educating their kiddos freely, without a school online or a bought homeschool curriculum, and by following their interests. And so can you.

If you decide to home-educate your children, you are responsible for evaluating their progress and explaining your children's growth and development to school officials or social workers who may not understand unschooling.

How can you test your children and create a report card?

You can mention in your home study plan and report that you will evaluate your children via observation. You can create a report card from scratch or use an online template. Since you are always observing your children, you can write "mastery" on the report card when you see them achieve a skill or milestone. Suppose your children are still not showing signs of certain skills. In that case, you can write "in progress," "emerging," or any other wording you prefer (mastering, advancing, progressing, emerging, beginning). Observing is a good way to test children's abilities.

Also, to report your children's progress, you can discuss it with your children, sort and categorize their achievements into academic subjects (I know, I'm sorry—you've been deschooling and now you have to think about school subjects again), and make the subjects align with your state requirements. It is also helpful to mention in the report that *unschooling*, *interest-led*, *natural curiosity-driven*, *intrinsic motivation*, or *self-directed* is your educational philosophy.

Self-directed education is a unique process that allows children to decide what, when, how, why, and from whom they want to learn. It can take some time, but it can also accelerate individual achievement. Therefore, if creating a report card is not working well with your kids' self-directed education, you can use a different evaluation method to capture the scope and sequence of self-directed learning.

Progress reports can also take the form of written narratives of your children's learning over a period, such as a quarter, half-year, or year. It is unnecessary to list every accomplishment, but you should provide one or two examples for each subject to describe your children's progress. Some families send an essay to school officials twice a year. They write long stories about what their kids have been up to in the previous six months.

Don't hesitate to be honest and transparent in your report, even if it means acknowledging differences in your children's progress compared to standardized school learning schedules, such as reading skills or formal math instruction. Explain that these differences are a thoughtful decision on your part. Taking a proactive approach instead of a defensive one can lead to positive outcomes. By presenting the absence of certain skills as a deliberate choice within your educational approach, school officials are more likely to see it as an alternative philosophy rather than neglect.

Make sure to show that you are aware of your children's challenges and recognize their importance. School officials may struggle to understand your perspective, so it's important to avoid any perception of neglect and provide clear explanations based on your educational beliefs. Emphasize that your children's delayed skills are an integral part of your approach, supported by studies and credible sources, to help them better understand and appreciate your approach.

Some families in other states must submit an Individualized Home Instruction Plan (IHIP) every year. These families have to report at the beginning of the year what they'll be teaching and report what their kids have learned at the end of the year. If you live in a high-regulation state, you can still educate by facilitating self-directed education. You can unschool and comply with the rules.

The IHIP form requires you to submit your children's names, ages, and grade levels. You must also submit a list of your syllabi, curriculum materials, textbooks, or plan of instruction; dates for submission of quarterly reports; and the name of whoever is giving the instruction.

A successful education, the kind in which kids guide their learning, is not easy to plan and put in a portfolio when you are just starting to educate your kids. An IHIP is detailed. How do you know in advance what your kids will be learning? Here's what you can do if you have to show every year to the state your kids are learning but you don't have anything planned because you don't know where your kids' interests will take you.

Document every activity you do the year before sending mandatory reports and try to categorize it into a school subject. Make a list of all the stuff you do—travels, outings, projects, experiences, books read, conversations had, movies, shows, documentaries, whatever! Start by writing what your kids are learning/doing/exploring/playing every week, and try to put everything into categories that roughly coincide with the required subjects. At the end of the year, you'll have a portfolio!

Now, use this portfolio and change it slightly to turn it into your next year's lesson plans. You can also write down any ideas of activities you want to expose your children to regardless of their interests. Write down any events your city might offer and events your library or museums might offer. Mention on your IHIP that you are providing your students with an outline of likely courses of study or activities. Just be sure to note that these are all subject to change and that you will provide detailed quarterly reports stating what was actually accomplished. As long as you are providing some detail, it will be fine, even if all of it changes for your quarterly reports.

Quarterly reports follow the same format as your IHIP, except you will write everything your children have done. Keep a list or take pictures of things your kids do. Every day or every week, make a few notes. Conversations with your children are also worth writing down. They are as important and valuable as any classes or field trips. It's all valid, and everything counts on reports. I'm sure you'll find yourself with too much info rather than an insufficient amount. Quarterly reports should not be more than two pages. The employees getting them do not want to wade through many pages. They want to be able to take a glance and check their boxes.

After a few years, it will get easier to write yearly reports. Some families have a private Instagram account to record their children's learning and invite the home study case worker to check it when it's time for the annual report. And some families let their kids write their own reports. They are the ones who know what they have learned and where they want to go, and you get to see how well they write.

Here's some vocabulary if you need help translating what your kids do into a report.

- Reading the Daily Paper or online news = Current Events, Social Studies
- Playing Monopoly = Math
- Genealogy = History, Language Arts
- Cooking = Math, Science
- Any Martial Arts, Sports, Rock Climbing = Physical Education
- Talking with Grandpa about His Life = History
- Photography = Science, Art
- Chess = Critical Thinking
- Climbing Trees = Physical Education, Science
- Visiting Museums = History, Science, Fine Arts
- Appliance Repair = Science
- Catalogs = Math and Reading

- Fiction = Contemporary Literature
- Nonfiction = Science, History, Language Arts
- Playing Restaurant and Writing the Pretend Menu= Writing Language Arts
- Reading Information at Each Habitat at the Zoo= Reading Language Arts, Science

If you need to get familiar with or need a guide for the education wording, you can easily learn by getting a cheap complete curriculum workbook for your children's grade or go to a website like ixl.com or worldbook.com and use them to see how to classify things your child already knows or is in the process of learning.

Math:
- Learning to tell the day and time
- Counting, stacking, or lining up objects
- Using measuring cups and spoons while cooking
- Measuring using a measuring tape
- Playing chess, card games or other games of strategy
- Using the calendar

Geometry, art, architecture, and engineering:
- Playing with blocks, LEGOs, and other building toys

Chemistry:
- Cooking and other fun experiments

Hands-on Science:
- Forming hypotheses and testing them out
- Making lab notes of experiments

Language arts:
- Reading, writing, or being read to and creating stories
- Watching movies or plays based on books

Film studies:
- Watching movies with original screenplays

Computer science:
- Building a website, designing an app, programming a robot, or building a computer
- Helping others with technology, such as teaching family members how to use new apps

Economics, marketing, and business math:
- Starting a business or selling products

Practical arts:
- Baking, cooking, or repairing objects around the house
- Decorating cupcakes, styling a room, sewing costumes, designing and constructing furniture or other objects

Nature study:
- Walking through parks or collecting specimens, such as identifying trees, plants, or tadpoles

Biology:
- Observing worms or other living organisms

Astronomy:
- Observing comets, shooting stars, or other celestial objects

Physics:
- Playing with toy trucks or visiting construction sites

- Building roller coasters for marbles or building ramps for cars or skateboarding

Field trips:
- Visiting tourist attractions, bakeries, firehouses, television studios, farms, or factories

Art history:
- Touring art museums or galleries

Urban planning and geography:
- Walking around town and noting outdoor sculptures, murals, and architectural landmarks

Current events:
- Discussing news stories

Social studies:
- Reading social studies magazines and books, attending Memorial Day services, or accompanying parents in voting booths

Physical education:
- Dancing, walking, swimming, biking, or running around on the lawn

When your kids get older, writing an education plan and report to show to your state's Department of Education case worker will be easier. Your kids will be so focused on the plan they have in mind that they will execute it no matter what. Learning from life and following their interests and passions without using a formal and traditional educational curriculum for high school prepares students for college and beyond.

If you reach middle or high school age, and your children have never learned a mandatory subject that the state requires them to learn, explain to your children that the state mandates learning this subject. If your state requires learning a specific subject that your kids have zero interest in and life has never brought that lesson, brainstorm together ways to make it easier for your children to learn the subject. Would it be watching a series of YouTube videos? Listening to a series of podcasts? Reading a certain book? Attending a class? Work with your children to determine what best fits them. Discuss their goals, likes, strengths, and weaknesses, and then work with them to set a plan.

And some families either like to test or have no choice but to test their children. A list of accepted tests is given on your state's Department Of Education website on the homeschooling info page. These tests can be ordered online by many companies and administered at home under calm conditions.

If you need help, you can hire an unschooling coach online or find an unschooling website for your state or country. What truly helps is learning from veteran families who have successfully educated their children and became experts in submitting their IHIPs, quarterly reports, and annual assessments without issues for years. Join a group of homeschooling families or a homeschool co-op and discover who the unschooling or child-led families are. They'll tell you all the tricks and loopholes.

Remember, If you want to give your children a successful education but strict government requirements scare you, you can use an umbrella school. A lot of families feel safer that way. They join these schools because they want the added peace of mind and guidance the umbrella program can provide them. The umbrella program offers assistance and fulfills state educational requirements, material needed, testing services, transcripts, attendance records, and other helpful documentation.

And, of course, if you want to provide a successful education to your children but can't or don't want to educate them at home, you can enroll them in a democratic school or a self-directed learning center.

Requiring children to constantly prove their learning is harming education. Cramming, memorizing, and studying for a test do not equate to true learning. Genuine learning involves a deeper understanding and retention of knowledge rather than just memorization for a test. However, suppose your kids' path (going to college, getting certified, getting a driver's license, etc.) requires taking a test. In that case, your self-directed learners will study and pass without harming their learning motivation.

You can find a sample of an Education Plan and a sample of a Progress Report at ahem.info. Sample progress reports and a sample report card are on the following pages.

PROGRESS REPORT

HOME EDUCATION

Student Name: _____
School Year: _____
Grade: _____
Semester: _____

SUBJECT LIST	COMMENTS
Language Arts	
Reading	
Math	
Geometry	
Earth Science	
Social Studies	
Art	

INTERESTS	COMMENTS
music	
horse riding	
animals	

HOME EDUCATION

PROGRESS REPORT

SY 20___-___

STUDENT'S NAME: _____   GRADE: _____

TOTAL CLASS DAYS: _____   DAYS PRESENT: _____   DAYS ABSENT: _____   QUARTER: _____

	GRADE	COMMENTS
MATH		
SCIENCE		
HISTORY		
ENGLISH		
SOCIAL STUDIES		
GYM		
ART		
MUSIC		

AVERAGE QUARTERLY GRADE: _____   AVERAGE OVERALL GRADE: _____

GRADING SCALE:

A+ = 97%-100%	B+ = 87%-89%	C+ = 77%-79%	D+ = 67%-69%
A = 94%-96%	B = 84%-86%	C = 74%-76%	D = 64%-66%
A- = 90%-93%	B- = 80%-83%	C- = 70%-73%	D- = 60%-63%
			F- 59% BELOW

Weekly Progress Report

Name: _____ Date: _____

Behavior:	Study/Work Habits:
❏ Excellent ❏ Very Good ❏ Good ❏ Needs improvement ❏ Unsatisfactory	❏ Works independently and completes all work. ❏ Needs some assistance but completes work. ❏ Needs much assistance and takes too long to complete work. ❏ Gets distracted easily and does not complete work. •• ❏ Puts forth much effort and does work neatly. ❏ Does not put forth effort and does work carelessly.

Math:	Reading:
❏ Excellent ❏ Very Good ❏ Good ❏ Needs improvement ❏ Unsatisfactory	❏ Excellent ❏ Very Good ❏ Good ❏ Needs improvement ❏ Unsatisfactory

Writing:	
❏ Excellent ❏ Very Good ❏ Good ❏ Needs improvement ❏ Unsatisfactory	_____ *Parent Signature* Comments:

REPORT CARD

Name: Year:

Class: Date:

Subject	1st	2nd	3rd	4th	Average

Attendance	Number
Days Present	
Excused Absences	
Unexcused Absences	
Total Absences	

Whenever we prevent our kids from playing or exploring in the ways they prefer, we place another brick in a barrier between them and us. We are saying, in essence, "I don't trust you to control your own life." Children are suffering today not from too much computer play or too much screen time. They are suffering from too much adult control over their lives and not enough freedom.

—Peter Gray

SCREEN TIME

THROUGHOUT HISTORY, MANY ACTIVITIES THAT are now considered wholesome and educational were once viewed as harmful. For example, reading books was once considered a dangerous activity that could lead to moral corruption and anti-social behavior. Playing chess was viewed as a sinful and distracting activity that could lead people away from God. Yoga and meditation were once viewed as strange and exotic. They were associated with Eastern religions that were not widely understood. Dancing, throughout history, has been associated with various forms of sinfulness and immorality and has been banned in many cultures.

However, as time passed and people became more educated and open-minded, these views began to change. People began to recognize the value of these activities. For example, reading is now viewed as a way to expand your knowledge and imagination. As a result, these activities are now not only accepted but encouraged.

Today, we see a similar shift in attitudes toward screens and technology. Many parents are wary of allowing children to spend too much time on devices such as phones, tablets, and computers, fearing they may harm their children's social and cognitive development. However, it's important to remember that screens are not inherently bad or harmful. Like any tool, they can be used for good or for ill. When used responsibly and in moderation, screens can be a powerful tool for learning, creativity, and communication.

For example, screens can be used to access a wealth of information and resources that might not be available otherwise, connect with others worldwide, and create and share art, music, and other forms of expression. Additionally, many educational games and apps can help children develop important skills such as problem-solving, critical thinking, and creativity.

While some parents still view screens with suspicion, screens are rapidly becoming an essential part of modern life. Like reading books, screens have the potential to be a valuable tool for learning and growth as long as they are used in a responsible and balanced way. Of course, ensuring children use screens safely and responsibly is important. This means setting appropriate guidance for on-screen use and teaching children about the risks associated with online activity. Just like you teach your kids to cross the street, not talk to strangers, stay safe in a swimming pool, and not get lost at the shopping mall, take the same approach with the internet. Slowly practice with your kids, educate them, and practice again until you see your kids are mature enough to navigate independently.

I was also concerned about screens and the internet and how many TV shows my kids watched. Then came the iPads, smartphones, and social media, which were very new to me. Allowing my kids to navigate the internet was scary. I am the kind of parent and educator who thinks kids need to play in nature as much as possible. However, I am also very aware that screens are a part of our lives, and the amount of information you can get in just a second is outstanding. You can now take a picture of an insect or a leaf from your nature adventure using your smartphone and find its name, type, and more facts. I call that learning! Screens are fantastic tools for learning, and if we limit them, we limit learning.

As technology becomes increasingly prevalent in our daily lives, the amount of time children spend on electronic screens has become a concern for many parents. There is a worry that excessive use may lead to addiction and a lack of self-control if not properly managed. To address this, many parents set rules and limits for screen time. But before you decide, I would like to help you understand the psychological impact of screen use on children.

Humans require autonomy, competency, and relatedness to stay motivated and fulfilled, just like you need food and water to survive. Neglecting these needs can result in a decline in mental well-being, much like depriving our bodies of sustenance can harm our physical health. Hence, it's vital to prioritize and foster these aspects in your children's lives to maintain optimal mental health.

Many children lack crucial experiences like autonomy, competency, and relatedness in their real-world lives and resort to seeking alternatives online. This leads to extended periods spent on the internet as they cannot find these essential components in their immediate physical environment.

Children who attend traditional schools or follow a rigorous homeschool curriculum with one parent being authoritarian, often experience a lack of autonomy in their daily lives. They have limited choices and are directed on what to do, think, and wear based on strict rules. However, when these children have the opportunity to go online, they find a sense of freedom and autonomy. They can freely explore their interests, make their own decisions, and encounter minimal adult control and surveillance.

Children who are educated following a standardized curriculum, whether in traditional or home-based schools, may have difficulty experiencing competency due to their diverse personalities and learning styles. Expecting all children to learn the same way or fit into a rigid mold is unrealistic. In contrast, children online have the freedom to explore and learn about topics that interest them, which can empower them to teach themselves new subjects and increase their confidence in their ability to learn independently. Additionally, many children turn to video games designed to provide a sense of achievement and competency.

Contrary to popular belief, children lack opportunities to develop social skills and make friends in school. They have limited time to socialize, play, connect, and relate. On the other hand, the internet provides a platform to find like-minded individuals, akin to a vast playground where people can connect over shared interests. Children can build friendships and socialize freely through online play, spending hours exploring games and working on self-selected projects. The internet and social media have become the park where teens hang out.

The rise of technology has led to a new form of addiction: screen addiction. Many people argue that the problem lies in the screens themselves. Still, the screen is not the problem, but the person's level of happiness and fulfillment in their daily lives. Addiction is a complex issue that can manifest in a variety of ways.

When someone struggles with addiction, it's often because they're seeking something they're missing in their life or trying to avoid. In the case of screens, addiction is typically related to a lack of autonomy, competency, and relatedness in the addicts' daily lives. When these needs aren't being met daily, it's easy to turn to screens as a source of fulfillment. Social media, video games, and other online activities provide a sense of control, a feeling of accomplishment, and a sense of connection to others. However, this can quickly spiral into addiction as the people increasingly rely on screens for their happiness and fulfillment.

So, what's the solution? Rather than simply limiting screen time, addressing the underlying issues driving the addiction is important. Providing children with opportunities to experience autonomy, competency, and relatedness in their daily lives can diminish their need to seek experiences online, ultimately leading to less screen time.

This can take many forms, from giving children more control over their daily routines to providing them with opportunities to develop new skills and hobbies. Encouraging social activities, whether playing with friends or joining a sports team, can also help foster a sense of connection and belonging. By addressing these needs in healthy, positive ways, children are less likely to turn to screens as a source of fulfillment, and the risk of addiction is greatly diminished.

Suppose you're concerned that screens may become an unhealthy obsession. In that case, you can guide your children by engaging in open discussions about the advantages and disadvantages of technology. Rather than imposing strict rules that may lead to frustration and resistance, explaining the costs and benefits of screen time can help children understand and help them develop the skills to make informed decisions about their tech use even when unsupervised.

It's important to be aware of potential dangers associated with digital resources and take steps to protect your children. As a media mentor, you can guide your children in using social media safely and responsibly. Educate them about risks such as sexual abuse, child pornography, and sex trafficking, and help them understand how to avoid dangerous situations online.

Set a positive example for your children by using technology responsibly and discussing the influence of social media influencers on their followers. Empowering children to make their own decisions is crucial instead of solely relying on others' opinions. Encourage them to verify the information before accepting it as true. Teach them how to navigate the internet safely by developing critical thinking skills. With these tools, children can confidently and securely navigate the digital world.

Provide opportunities to engage in the physical world by exploring different hobbies, organizing playdates with friends, and offering exciting outdoor experiences and trips. Children will be less likely to miss their screens if you create meaningful and fulfilling family time. Encouraging a balance between screen time and other activities can help you feel more at ease when your children use screens, knowing they have had diverse experiences beyond technology. And instead of focusing on limiting screen time, spend quality time with your children and observe their screen use without judgment. Screens can allow your family to connect with your children and engage in activities they enjoy. It's important to recognize that for some young people, screens offer unique benefits that may not be available elsewhere.

Don't blame screen time or video games for your children's unhappiness; do not assume banning screens will improve your children's well-being. Instead, you must identify the root of their unhappiness, as gaming is rarely the root cause of their problems. Addressing the underlying issues can help your children feel happier and more fulfilled without giving up something they enjoy. Value your children's joy, curiosity, and exploration, even if it involves screen time. Hating on screens means hating the things that bring your children happiness. Instead, try to join in on your children's interests, even if it's not your preference. By showing genuine interest and support, you demonstrate to your kids that you care about their passions and, most importantly, them.

The quality of screen time is more important than the quantity. You may inadvertently limit your child's opportunities to learn and grow by overly restricting technology usage. New technologies offer numerous interactive and engaging learning opportunities to enhance children's education and study effectiveness. Setting limits on technology use can increase your children's desire for it. Restricting access may lead to binging, hyper-focusing, anxiety, or sneaking around. Moreover, when children are finally allowed to use technology, they don't fully enjoy it because they fear it will be taken away. Your boundaries create an illusion of control without actually providing guidance. Developing a positive relationship with your children can be more effective in guiding and educating them. Limiting anything undermines trust. Instead, ask your kids why they like that game, YouTube channel, or app so much. Listen and be amazed. Do not presume that certain activities are less valuable than others. Video gaming, YouTubing, and social media also lead to learning. Spend time with your children online and learn to value what they value.

As a parent, it's up to you to decide what types of play are appropriate for your children. Some parents choose not to allow their kids to play with sticks or climb trees, while others may prohibit playing with toy guns. It's your decision based on what you believe is best for your children. This also applies to screen time, electronic devices, and video gaming. Ultimately, it's up to you to decide what role these things should play in your children's life. I can tell you that our decisions are often based on our own experiences, education, and environment. It's natural to fear the unknown; many of us may be wary of things we don't fully understand. For instance, you may have grown up without social media, apps, and video games. In contrast, children today are surrounded by technology from an early age. It's important to recognize that our childhoods and experiences are different. What worked for us may not necessarily work for our children.

Regardless of whether your kids have screen access when they are young or when your kids are older, it is crucial to help them learn the concepts of media use. Instead of being afraid, learn all the rules with them to ensure safety. Children require adult mentorship that teaches them not to blindly surrender to influences and encourages them to become critical thinkers. They need to develop technology and internet literacy skills. Think of electronic devices, the internet, video games, and social media like a swimming pool. Kids have a blast playing in the pool, exercising, socializing, learning, and having great family time. However, some kids can get hurt, drown, get lost, be bullied, and experience theft. Some pools have lifeguards to protect the swimmers, and some don't. Similarly, as you teach your children to swim and stay safe and based on the maturity and skills of your children, you make decisions about wearing a floating device or allowing them to swim in the deep end. You should do the same with the digital world.

Also, whenever you get irritated or concerned because your children have been in front of an electronic device for hours and you want them to stop, ask yourself, would you stop your children if they were sitting down reading a book for hours? Or laying down on the floor playing with LEGOs all day?

I don't have a problem with screens and video games, but I don't actively encourage them. They are just other tools for learning and helpful supplements. And like any other activity, I base my decisions on my budget and my children's level of maturity. What concerns you the most about electronics—the possibility of promoting solitude and isolation? Reading books can also promote solitude and isolation. Are you worried that technology might take over your children's lives? Technology is a tool, and you and your kids control how you use it. Your children are in control, not the other way around. Could it be that you are afraid of electronics because it is something unfamiliar to you? Perhaps you didn't grow up with them. Consider learning together with your children.

I have had prior experience with video games, as my brother and I played them during our teenage years. However, my brother played more than I did. I also know many successful adults who played video games when they were kids and continue to play as adults. I have always had a positive image of video gaming. On the other hand, I was unfamiliar with social media and felt uneasy about my kids using those apps. I expressed my concerns to my kids, and we had open discussions about the potential risks, learning about them together.

For some children, playing video games may be the only area where they feel competent and confident. Others may struggle with social interactions due to isolation or bullying and find solace in online gaming as a way to connect with others. In such cases, online gaming can be a valuable tool for building relationships and boosting self-esteem. Many video games are challenging and require time to master, allowing children to develop skills and gain confidence. Limiting screen time limits free play, which is an important part of learning. Video games can also foster artistic expression and creative thinking, skills valuable for future career prospects.

Social media offers significant advantages. Even though it has its negative aspects, such as cyberbullying and spreading false information, it allows us to connect with others, stay informed, and share our perspectives and experiences with a global audience. It can also provide opportunities for networking, self-expression, and community-building.

I used to be concerned about my kids spending too much time in front of screens, but I was curious to see what would happen if they had complete screen time freedom. Surprisingly, I discovered that they could self-regulate and balance their time effectively. It works. When kids know they can use electronics without restrictions, they balance their time with other activities. Offer them activities like going to the pool, hiking, riding bikes, playdate, anything outside the house, or something as simple as playing in the front yard with the neighbors or a board game. They will choose the other activities if they know they can use electronics any time without any worries. Even if they play on screens for extended periods, it's fine, too, as it means they are trying to achieve something in that game. Take the time to sit down with them and learn about the game they are playing. You might be surprised at how wonderful some games can be.

Instead of focusing solely on restricting your children's screen time, prioritize monitoring the content they consume, as it has a greater impact. Digital media offers significant advantages, including convenient access to information, education, and employment opportunities.

The biggest enemy to learning is the talking teacher.

—John Holt

TEACHERS

As a former teacher, I find John Holt's opinion on teachers accurate. But please do not take offense. Instead, remind yourself to continuously educate yourself on how children learn. By reading and searching for knowledge on this subject, you can gain valuable insights and approaches to better support your students. I highly recommend reading some books by John Holt or John Taylor Gatto, both teachers. Peter Gray's *Free to Learn* and Naomi Fisher's *Changing Our Minds* are also great resources. Teachers need to learn about how children learn best.

Choosing a teaching method that is convenient for you may not be convenient for your students. To facilitate the best learning, it's important to let the learner take charge. Teachers, it's essential to adapt to your student's needs and not force them to adapt to your teaching style. Every student is unique, and you must select the best approach for them. You have a challenging job, and it's crucial to prioritize your students' learning above all else.

Most of us, including myself, deviated from the natural way of raising children. I invite you to join me and other educators in embracing a new (actually old) way of educating children and adolescents. Children are naturally wired to learn, and all they need is the freedom to do so. Let's give them that space.

Kids, teens, and adults learn and work better when they control their actions. Intrinsic motivation beats extrinsic motivation over and over again. Kids are naturally hungry for knowledge. Our job is to nurture their interests, guide their curiosity, facilitate their explorations, and give them the space to explore and grow. And most importantly, get out of their way.

Anyone who has spent quality time with young children knows their innate drive to learn is fueled by their interests and fascinations. Neglecting to acknowledge children's interests and prior experiences when teaching young children can be frustrating for everyone involved. It can result in missed valuable learning opportunities.

Meeting all of your student's interests can be challenging, but it is achievable by creating a well-resourced, enabling environment. It is essential to show children that their environment is safe, fun, and interesting, encouraging them to explore and learn.

Perspective is the art of seeing things. It is the way we look at those same things differently. Teacher, please, look at education differently. Much of the current effort in education is spent attempting to motivate students to learn. You are exhausted because you are going against the natural current, against the nature of your students, and against how children naturally learn. Your students are already motivated to learn, but you are teaching content they are not interested in or don't see the value of.

Most of your students do not want to be in your class and are not interested in what you are teaching.

Many educators today struggle to motivate their students to learn. But the problem is not with the students. It is the way we approach education. As a teacher, you can shape the learning experience and create an environment that fosters curiosity and engagement. Instead of teaching to a standardized curriculum, personalize your lessons to match your students' interests and learning styles. By seeing education through a different lens, you can help your students thrive. Create a student-centered classroom where students have a say in what they learn and how they learn. You can tap into their curiosity and inspire them to become lifelong learners.

Schools are unfocused because kids are not learning from their own motivation but rather forced to learn subjects that may be of no interest or use to them. Let's try to turn your class into focused learning, where kids are motivated to learn subjects they are passionately interested in by their own free will, so they pick up and learn things much faster.

Instead of just giving facts and knowledge and testing students on how well they remember them, try giving them the freedom to explore and discover the information they need or want. Since students must be in your class and you must teach them certain standards, find ways to incorporate their interests and passions into the curriculum. This will help them engage with the material and learn it more deeply.

How can you personalize their learning and help your students pass your class?

To personalize your student's learning, you must tailor the instructional environment to each student's needs and interests. Learning accelerates when choosing what, when, how, and where to learn. Be transparent with your students. Explain to them that you are responsible for teaching certain standards they need to learn to graduate. However, offer them flexibility in learning those standards and when. Give them the freedom to explore and acquire knowledge through different channels, such as watching a YouTube video, reading a book, listening to a podcast, or following your lesson plan. Allow them to demonstrate their learning in a way that suits their interests and strengths, whether taking a test, writing an essay, completing a project, or doing a presentation. This way, they can take ownership of their learning and feel more motivated to engage with the material.

You don't have to teach if you provide the conditions in which children can learn. You can design your classroom, even middle and high school classrooms, with various learning centers, much like a kindergarten class. Instead of being a talking teacher, consider transitioning into the role of a guidance counselor. Your role is to inform students of the required standards and knowledge to be learned by the end of the year or semester while allowing them to choose how and when they want to learn. And be present for those who require extra assistance or wish to discuss the subject with you.

If your students' goal is to attend a prestigious

university and they are eager to learn and earn extra credits, embrace it and have fun with them. However, suppose students plans to enter a profession where your teaching subject is not applicable. In that case, it's important to be flexible and understanding. Allow the students to choose the most suitable approach to pass your class.

My youngest son is currently attending ninth grade in a public high school. Unfortunately, he has encountered a few toxic teachers with zero knowledge of connecting with their students. However, I would prefer not to focus on the negative aspects of the education system but rather share a positive experience my son had with a smart and knowledgeable educator.

My son's English teacher, known for his strictness, tried to connect with my son and understand his strengths and weaknesses. Through an honest conversation, my son could explain that he was placed in an English honors class without his consent and would prefer a regular English class as literature is not his passion. Instead, his interests lie in finances and business.

To my son's surprise, the teacher agreed to help him pass the class by adapting the work assignments and instead gave him a book to read along with a questionnaire to answer. This teacher rearranged and adapted the educational plan and demonstrated a willingness to listen and provide his students with what they need to succeed.

I hope you will consider and try this powerful approach. Personalized and self-directed learning empowers students to make informed decisions about their learning. It grants them the freedom to choose what they want to learn and the pace at which they want to learn it, leading to a more customized and engaging learning experience. Managing personalized learning in a large class can be challenging. Still, thanks to advancements in technology, it is becoming more manageable to make the learning process more efficient and effective.

Create a comfortable learning environment for your students. Inspire them and let their creativity and talents shine. Support and understand them so you can communicate with them effectively and find the right approach for their learning needs. Personalized learning allows you to connect meaningfully with your students, and strong relationships with them will help facilitate their learning.

Cultivate intrinsic motivation in your students by granting them autonomy over their learning journey. Rather than being directed on what to learn, let them have the freedom to choose from a set of options that align with their interests and goals. This personal connection to the subject matter sparks an inherent drive to succeed, as students are naturally motivated by what is meaningful to them.

What I'm daring you to do is not new; it's already been done in some schools with wonderful results. Students can choose how their environment operates, with whom to interact, and if, how, and when to be evaluated. This personalized approach is radically different from any other form of education, and it's what sets successful education apart.

*F*ar too many people believe that the only way to teach a child is to force him to do something, or to give him rewards for doing it. But there are other ways far more pleasant, far more respectful of the child as a human being, and far more likely to lead to cooperation and growth.

—John Holt

NAVIGATING THE STORM

IF YOU ARE READING THIS BOOK, YOU ARE likely a parent who practices conscious and mindful parenting. Many parents who desire to facilitate self-directed education and unschool their children are led to do so by conscious parenting. However, for some of us, it is unschooling that has guided us toward conscious parenting. These two concepts are undoubtedly intertwined and complement each other.

I used to be an authoritarian parent—not by choice, but because it was the only approach I knew. Thankfully, when my children were nine, seven, and five years old, I discovered the unschooling lifestyle. Without realizing it and without any knowledge of conscious and mindful parenting, I inevitably became a mindful parent. I never read books or listened to any podcasts about conscious parenting. However, my desire to give my children a successful education remarkably transformed me into a respectful parent. Unschooling transforms your kids' education and your relationship with your children, and it changes you. It even improves your marriage!

While the terms "conscious parenting" and "mindful parenting" are often used interchangeably, there are some differences between the two approaches. Conscious parenting emphasizes the importance of self-awareness and personal growth in parenting. It encourages you to examine your beliefs, attitudes, and behaviors and work on your personal development to be better equipped to parent consciously and intentionally.

Mindful parenting, on the other hand, focuses on being present and fully engaged in the parenting experience. It involves paying close attention to your thoughts, feelings, and physical sensations at the moment and being fully attuned to your children's needs and experiences. Both approaches share a common goal of promoting positive and intentional parenting, but they approach it from slightly different angles. Conscious parenting focuses more on personal growth and development, while mindful parenting emphasizes being present and engaged.

If you want to know how to discipline your children and deal with problems, here is some information about navigating the storm.

It's important to know that bad behavior is not your children being bad. It's a form of communication. Children act out when they feel overwhelmed, frustrated, or misunderstood, and it's up to you as a parent to listen, investigate, and try to understand what they are trying to express. Bad behavior is a red flag waving at you, letting you know something is not working. Pay attention and change. Connect with your children and create a safe space for open communication. Power struggles and bad behavior will disappear once you connect, and you'll be able to work together to address any underlying issues that may be causing negative behavior. When children feel heard and understood, they are more likely to respond positively and cooperate rather than resort to challenging behavior.

When raising your children, be present, self-aware, and attentive to their needs. Understand their unique personalities, interests, and developmental stages. This parenting style has become increasingly popular in recent years, and for a good reason: it works exceptionally well when children become teenagers.

Conscious parenting is a journey; cultivating this approach takes time and effort. But by following these tips, you can create a strong and healthy relationship with your child based on mutual respect, empathy, and understanding.

1. Stay present: Being present at the moment is essential for conscious parenting. Try to be fully engaged with your children, listen to what they say, and respond with empathy and understanding.

2. Practice self-awareness: To be a conscious parent, you must be self-aware. This means being mindful of your emotions and reactions and understanding how they might impact your children.

3. Foster open communication: Encourage open communication with your children and create

a safe space where they feel comfortable sharing their thoughts and feelings.

4. Be empathetic: Try to understand your children's perspective and show empathy towards their emotions, even if you don't agree with their actions.

5. Set boundaries: Setting clear boundaries and expectations is important for conscious parenting. This helps your children understand what is acceptable behavior and what is not.

6. Encourage independence: Give your children space to make their own decisions, and support them in their journey towards independence.

7. Focus on positive reinforcement: Rather than punishing negative behavior, focus on positive reinforcement for good behavior. This helps to build self-esteem and reinforces positive habits.

One of the reasons conscious parenting is so effective during adolescence is that it fosters a strong, trusting relationship between parents and children. Parents are often the primary source of comfort, guidance, and support when children are young. As children grow older, they become more independent and seek out their identities. During this time, it can be challenging for parents to maintain positive relationships with their children. However, conscious parenting can help parents navigate this period by building trust, open communication, and mutual respect.

Another reason conscious parenting is effective during adolescence is that it allows parents to understand teenagers' unique challenges. Adolescence is a time of intense change, both physically and emotionally. Teenagers often deal with peer pressure, academic stress, and social anxiety. Conscious parenting helps you understand these challenges and provides tools to help your children navigate them successfully.

Furthermore, conscious parenting promotes autonomy and self-reliance in children, which is particularly important during adolescence. Teenagers often strongly desire independence and autonomy, and conscious parenting encourages parents to support their children in this process. By allowing your children to make their own decisions and take responsibility for their actions, you can help them build a strong sense of self-confidence and self-esteem.

Conscious parenting is a powerful tool for raising teenagers. By building strong, trusting relationships with your children, understanding the unique challenges of adolescence, and promoting autonomy and self-reliance, you can help your children navigate this challenging period with confidence and success.

Conscious parenting is not a one-size-fits-all approach. It requires ongoing effort and attention. However, the benefits of this approach are clear: teenagers raised with conscious parenting are more likely to be emotionally healthy, confident, and successful in their personal and professional lives.

Allow your children and teens to unfold as they are, not as you wish them to be. Nurture them but let go of controlling them. Trust me.

True learning—learning that is permanent and useful, that leads to intelligent action and further learning—can arise only out of the experience, interest, and concerns of the learner.

—John Holt

DREAMS UNLEASHED

Release the script in your head of the life you had envisioned for your children, as it is ultimately their life to live. Avoid the urge to manipulate or orchestrate their paths; instead, allow them the freedom to choose how they want to live life.

Dreams lead kids places. When parents trust their kids to follow their dreams, lots and lots of learning happens. Don't crush your kids' dreams, even if you believe their aspirations are impossible. Allow their dreams to run their course and provide their own wake-up call. Let your kids learn for themselves that their goals may not be feasible rather than trying to redirect them. While parents may do this to protect their children from disappointment, not supporting them can be more harmful in the long run.

Dreams fuel people. Your children will learn valuable lessons as they pursue their goals. It's okay to feel concerned when your kids attempt something that may not turn out as expected. But remember that each experience is an opportunity for growth and learning. Unfortunately, parents' good intentions of shielding their children from disappointment can hinder kids from life's greatest joy of learning and being themselves.

It is more harmful to children when their parents do not provide support than allowing them to realize that their dream may not come true on their own. It is a more natural process for the dream to slowly reveal its limitations to the person over time. This approach allows children to better understand themselves and their goals, leading to greater growth and resilience.

If you are the parent of children with ambitious dreams—whether to become an artist, athlete, musician, or entrepreneur or to pursue a unique path—avoid crushing their aspirations. Resist the urge to let your fears and doubts influence them. Instead, allow life to shape their dreams over time. Encourage your kids to explore their interests and passions and offer support as they navigate the ups and downs of pursuing their goals.

Avoid crushing your children's aspirations; instead, place more trust in their abilities. Provide them with the necessary guidance and support to help them achieve their goals. If they encounter obstacles, encourage them to persevere and explore alternative paths. Remember that with your belief in their potential and unwavering support, your children can accomplish great things and find their true calling.

Many parents worry that if their children pursue their dreams, they will struggle financially or fail altogether. As a result, they push their children toward more conventional career paths, such as getting a college degree, rather than supporting them in following their passions.

While it is certainly important for children to have a solid education and career prospects, it is equally important for them to have the opportunity to pursue their dreams and interests. Forcing children to abandon their dreams in favor of a college degree or a more "practical" career can lead to feelings of resentment, frustration, and unfulfillment.

Parents afraid of their children pursuing dreams do so out of love and concern for their children's well-being. However, it is important to remember that children have unique passions, talents, and interests. By supporting your children in pursuing their dreams, you can help them develop the skills, confidence, and resilience they need to succeed in any path they choose.

If your children have dreams that you are hesitant to support, take the time to listen to their perspective and understand their motivations. Offer constructive feedback and guidance to help them achieve their goals rather than discourage them altogether. Encourage them to explore their interests and passions, and help them build the skills and connections they need to succeed.

Remember that success is not just measured by financial wealth or career status but also by personal fulfillment and happiness. You can help your children achieve a sense of purpose and joy that will last a lifetime by supporting your children in pursuing their dreams.

*C*hildren are not only extremely good at learning; they are much better at it than we are.

—John Holt

THE ORIGINAL WAY OF LEARNING

ONCE, SOMEONE ASKED ME WHAT I LOVED most about unschooling my children. I found it difficult to provide a specific answer because the experience has enriched me in every way. As an educator, I have learned so much from the process. As a parent, it has completely transformed my mindset and made me happier, more peaceful, and freer. Moreover, I have had the privilege of watching my children learn without any expectations or comparisons, pursuing their passions and ignoring outdated beliefs, and developing a strong sense of self not shaped by external influences like me, their father, or teachers. And the best part of it all is seeing the incredible results that come with time. Even after many years, I am still amazed at how responsible and intelligent my children have become.

I've been attached to the word UNSCHOOL since the day I read it in John Holt's book, in which he explains and encourages parents to avoid replicating school in their homes. It clicked in my head, made so much sense, and I loved it. However, it's a word that scares many people and gives the wrong impression. Know that you don't have to use that word, and you don't have to label your kids' education. Still, suppose you need to use a term. In that case, there are a variety of others you can use, such as home education; homeschooling without a curriculum; educating freely; child-led, self-directed, interest-led, personalized curriculum; naturally learning—anything you feel fits! If you think about it, these approaches all emphasize a return to the original and natural way of learning.

Don't let a scary word stop you. Name it whatever you want. The point is to avoid replicating school. Why? Because school is designed with a standard child in mind. Does that child even exist? An education designed before even meeting a child is disastrous. Our children need a tailored education. Only this way will it be successful.

Kids don't need school.

They need space to explore and time to think. If you control kids' learning, you are missing the entire point of learning. True, meaningful learning can't be micromanaged. It needs space to grow and breathe. Suppose you are having a difficult time educating your children. In that case, I encourage you to give them free time and let them try many activities. Eventually, they'll discover their talents and predilections. Change methods if there's crying, anger, frustration, and yelling while you're teaching your kid. Learning is fun, and kids want to learn.

Self-directed education is effective because the approach allows parents to respect the development readiness of their children. Remember, children innately learn. They only need time, space, support, and exposure to the world. Learning freely will make your children unique individuals. It will equip your children with a true essence that will help them through difficult times, and this education will allow them to find values that will guide them through life.

When children take ownership of their education, they assume responsibility for their lives. Their thirst for knowledge becomes insatiable, and they work diligently and strive for excellence. Witnessing this level of dedication and self-motivation is truly inspiring. And when your children feel seen and appreciated in their own essence, you empower them. Now you know the secret to success. Accept and love them as they are, and you'll see them become the greatest, most original version of themselves.

This change of mentality and different ways of educating will positively impact your life. Not only educationally but in everything you'll do. It will change the way you live, the way you think, and the way you look at the world.

I am writing the final pages of this book in Europe, far away from home, while my daughter is being interviewed and watched auditioning, performing her amazing skills on a rope. It's such an emotional day that I can't even visit the city. I much rather be here with you.

Dear reader, trust that your children can guide their

education and learn without being taught in the traditional school way. Trust that your kids' play will lead to learning, sparking their interests and passions and eventually leading them to their future careers. Replace the school-based curriculum with your children's curiosity.

Dear reader, trust and give your children autonomy and opportunities, exposing them to everything possible to become whatever they want. Many people have asked me, "How? But how? Tell us how?" I hope this book has helped you. It is quite difficult to give a step-by-step guide to unschool or facilitate self-directed education. There is no guide or curriculum to follow. That's the whole point. Your children are your guides. Each child is an individual curriculum to follow. Observe your children. They'll let you know what they need.

You don't know how this education journey will turn out. Be prepared for the unknown. It can be beautiful or perhaps brutally boring for you, but it will have a great ending. Now, focus on your children's goals and help them achieve what they want. I know it's scary to let go of what's normal. I've been there. I hope this book gives you the tools to trust your children will learn independently. They are waiting for you to let them. The benefits are so worth it.

I gave my daughter everything I could. Now it's time for her to fly solo. Do you want to find out if she got into college?

Turn the page . . .

YES!

NOW I'M THE MOM OF AN AUTHOR AND A professional aerialist. Who would have thought my boy would be an amazing novelist and my daughter a fantastic athlete? I can't wait to find out what my youngest child, the unschooler who went to high school, will do next.

*N*o one has to do anything in order to "socialize" the children, or make them take part in the life of the group. They are born social; it is their nature.

—John Holt

A SOCIAL MISFIT AND OTHER MYTHS

EDUCATING YOUR KIDS WITHOUT SCHOOL IS all about allowing them to become themselves. You are not sheltering them from the world. They are learning every day by living in it.

Let's talk about all the myths about home education.

Homeschool people are weird.

Weird but happy. I have a few observations on this topic.

1. There are children in traditional schools who are also "weird." These children respond to their weirdness in two ways: either by continuing to embrace their unique qualities, which leads them to be without friends or by pretending to be someone they are not in order to fit in and make friends, which causes them to hide their true selves and suffer.

2. How wonderful that children who are "different" or have unique qualities have the great

option to be educated at home, where they can feel free to be themselves without fear of ridicule or pressure to conform. And as many moms say, "I don't want school to erase my children's uniqueness."

3. If society doesn't accept "different" people and label them as weirdos, what does that say about socialization in school?

How do they socialize? How do they function in the real world when they grow up?

Numerous people assume that children will not learn to get along with others and will not develop good social skills if they are not enrolled in a school. They imagine that our kids are studying all the time at home, alone, without friends to play with.

Our children have more time to participate in activities outside the home and play with other kids because they don't spend seven hours a day in a classroom sitting at a desk. Also, they have more opportunities to interact with children who are not the same age. They play with and learn from people of all ages, genders, and interests.

To socialize means to participate in social activities, mix socially with others, and behave in a way that is acceptable to society. Your children will learn to do all that because the principle socializing environment is the family. Going to friends' parties and family events, attending classes, participating in sports, simply going out on the street, going to the grocery store, and basically by living every day life, your kids will learn to socialize because it happens organically by interacting with the people around them. The only way to not socialize is to grow up living on a desert island without any interactions.

Children learn social skills through a number of relationships with adults and children of varying ages. When our children meet for group activities, we parents are usually present and very involved. When problems arise, parents are readily available to step in and facilitate. This provides a vast number of opportunities for our children to observe adaptive social skills and to practice them. Because of this constant modeling and adult guidance, children gain social skills that allow them healthy, satisfying relationships with people of all ages and backgrounds.

It is impossible not to socialize if you live your everyday life in society. Every week you interact, converse, meet, mix, mingle, get together, and are sociable. The beauty of tailoring your kids' education is that you can also tailor their socialization. Some kids are happy with a tranquil social life, while others need an out-and-about, always-busy social life.

If what worries you is how they will make friends, don't worry, they will. Everybody's situation is different, but here is how kids make friends:
- Neighbors playing in the street
- Neighborhood park, pool, library
- Classes, courses, sports, clubs
- Summer, winter and spring break camps
- Volunteering in an organization
- Homeschool groups and coops
- Church or community center

- Find or create a community

You'll be surprised how versatile and socially adjusted your kids will be when you give them the opportunity to direct their education. They are self-confident and less peer dependent than traditionally schooled students. Forget the myth that children who don't attend school become weirdos and unsocialized. The socially awkward kid exists in every school and in every homeschool group.

A successful education provides your children the best socializing strategy there is. What better way to practice being social and to practice how to behave in your society than by being in it every day. When children grow up they function well because they have spent more time out in the world learning about it while bathing in it, instead of being trapped in a classroom.

During the pandemic, we saw that it was harmful for children to be home all day.

What we experienced during the pandemic was not unschooling, but confinement. Educating without school is not confinement. Quite the contrary! It involves learning at home, outside the home, and everywhere in the city and in the world. In fact, spending five days in school can be more confining than living life without school.

Locking children and young people in a place where there are no changes, nothing new to explore, where they need permission to use the bathroom or drink water, and where playtime is minimum is confinement. Human beings are curious, and confining them for eight hours every day in the same building for years is cruel.

What about college?

Yes, if a child is interested in pursuing a passion that leads to college, then the child will get into college. Universities do accept students who were educated without school. Many self-directed learners have been accepted to college without a problem because of their maturity, independent thinking skills, creativity, and strong academic preparation.

Find out the rules of the admissions process. Each college is different. Some already explain on their website how to apply if you are a home student. Create a high school transcript and help your kids study to pass the SAT and ACT. However, lots of colleges do not require that test anymore, and some make testing optional.

You can find examples of self-directed learners who went to college in *Unschooling to University* by Judy Arnall and at grownunschoolers.com.

Only rich people can stay at home to educate their kids. Working parents can't educate at home.

I wish I was rich! The truth is many families who educate at home have a very humble income.

No matter what your job is, where you work, or what your circumstances are, you can successfully educate your children at any age and prepare them for life, even if you are busy with your own career.

Many families work and educate their children at home. Families that own their own business, couples who schedule their work hours making sure there is always one parent home, parents who find remote jobs with flexible hours, freelancers, and entrepreneurs all do it. I have met hairdressers, clothing company owners, social media managers, editors and translators, online teachers, maple syrup business owners, candle makers, eBay sellers, truck business owners, authors and speakers, chefs, airport workers, and nurses who successfully educate their kids without school.

And then there are parents whose jobs are demanding and don't have flexible hours such as lawyers and doctors. Those families hire a nanny, a retired teacher, or a homeschool mom to take care of their children, and other families choose to enroll their kids in self-directed education centers.

Be creative in finding resources. Ask your job if you can work from home or find and hire someone who will cherish your children's curiosity about life, people, and how things work and will respect their constant exploring. Hire someone who understands the job requirement to guide children and provide the resources and environment they need to continue this lifelong pursuit of knowledge.

Back in the day, families used to help each other by taking turns taking care of each other's kids while parents had to go to work. Now families count on a variety of business support such as civic centers, micro schools, and learning pods. Or self-directed learners can hang out at beautiful places such as moonrise.com, where you can drop your kids off several days a week.

But, letting children do whatever they want is not good. They need to learn to do things they don't want to do; it's part of life. They can't spend all day playing and doing what they want.

That's true, doing things we don't want to do is part of life. And as I've said before, growing up without school is living life; therefore, we will come across activities that we don't want to do. Children learn to do things they don't want to do, such as going to bed when they would rather play, washing their hands, taking a shower, brushing their teeth, picking up their toys, and eating healthy. There are many things they don't want to do, but they do them because we are educating them.

For example, when my children were young, I told them that I was tired of washing everyone's dishes and that they should wash their own after eating. For years now, they have been washing their own dishes. Of course, they don't want to do it, but they do it. The same goes for the laundry; all three of them wash their own clothes. It's not something they want to do, but it's necessary. When their father went to work in Afghanistan for a long time, they didn't want him to leave, but they coped and got used to something they didn't want. And during the years they worked at the equestrian center, they didn't want to clean up horse manure every day, but they did it so they could ride horses.

They learn to do things they don't feel like doing, and they do them because they are necessary. For example, my daughter didn't feel like training in gymnastics moves on the floor, but she had to in order to pass the first set of tryouts to audition for circus arts college. It was frustrating, difficult and unfair, but she did it. My son's friend didn't want to study math, but he did it to pass the college entrance exam. And my youngest son doesn't feel like going to high school every day and listening to some toxic teachers, but he's putting up with it in order to experience varsity high school soccer.

And then there are the challenges that life gives you. The most recent one, the pandemic and its confinement, taught us all to do things we didn't want to do. My children had planned to spend the summer of 2020 in Spain with my family, but the pandemic arrived and ruined their plans. Two years later, my daughter, who didn't want to get vaccinated against COVID-19, did it so she could go to Spain and visit her grandmother. Following your passions and learning what you enjoy does not prevent you from learning to do things you don't like. Life gives you many difficulties, enough to learn that sometimes you have to do what you don't want to do.

But it's equally essential to learn to say *NO*. It's important to have the freedom to say "No, I don't want to." It's important to have the freedom to choose not to do something and to leave an activity that no longer interests you.

I'm not smart enough to educate my children.

I've heard these words so many times from people who went to school and believe they are not intelligent enough. Don't make the mistake of sending your children to the same school system that, according to you, did not make you smart.

If you don't know much and you believe you're not intelligent, don't worry! You will learn along with your kids. I didn't know much about history, so my son taught me. He still teaches me. You don't need to be super smart. Believe me, you are qualified to educate your children because you are not going to indoctrinate them, but rather enhance their intellectual development. The important thing is not to be very intelligent, but to be resourceful and creative with the solutions you will need during the process to provide for their needs. It is essential to be honest and humble and to learn together. I have told my children thousands of times, "I don't know, I have no idea. Let's find out."

I'm afraid.

Of course, you're afraid. We've been conditioned to think that kids can only learn in school and that parents don't know how to educate their children. But don't be afraid to educate your kids outside of the school system. Instead, be afraid of sending them to a failing system that's letting down so many children.

Read as many articles as you can on self-directed education, attend conferences or listen to podcasts on unschooling, talk to other knowledgeable families, and read books on this topic to develop your confidence. Fear will disappear when you have deschooled your mind.

Every time you feel scared or doubt arises remember

this: Learning is innate in humans. It does not need to be manipulated, because learning is something your kids want and love to do. When you allow your children to learn naturally, on their own terms, by answering their curiosity and providing opportunities to pursue their interests, beautiful things happen. Change your thinking, forget the idea that a five-year-old child should already know the alphabet, forget that in second grade they should spell words correctly, forget that in fifth grade they are supposed to learn fractions, forget that going to college is better than working in a supermarket. Forget all this. Children can learn anything they put their minds to in a short period of time at an older age, quickly and easily. And not going to college is not the end of the world; on the contrary, it is the beginning of a new world.

Calm down, trust the process, trust that children learn. Trust your instincts. Try it. You have nothing to lose by giving it a shot. Keep in mind that if your children, for some reason, need to learn all academic subjects, it only takes a year or two to do so.

Many people think that children have to attend school and work hard on homework and projects to succeed in life. This is not true for everyone. Do you want school to teach your children passively and for them to forget everything they learned in a few months? Or do you want your children to love learning and always learn with pleasure, and retain everything they learn?

Children learn a lot simply by living life, and when they have the freedom to play and self-direct their learning they become non-stop learning machines. School is not necessary. What's necessary for working families is to have their children go somewhere while parents go to work, but where kids go nowadays is not educational. It's a place that extinguishes the curiosity of children and their desire to learn.

We have forgotten the natural way of raising children. Old ways are the new way. Not schooling children is not a strange or radical idea. On the contrary, it is something that humans have done for a long time. Leaving your children in the hands of strangers who indoctrinate them is what's strange and radical.

It is also radical to segregate children by age. If teachers, school principals, and education officials knew about education, they would know how important it is to mix ages to benefit learning. It is also radical to put pressure on students to do things perfectly. This anxiety makes learning difficult, and as a result, many children are labeled with "learning disorders." Assessments, expectations, and inhibition all affect learning. It is outrageous to label so many children unfavorably.

It is strange to me that educators do not know that freedom and opportunity are keys to education. It is rare that they do not know that playing is the best way to develop personal responsibility, self-control, and sociability, which are natural ways of learning for humans. Don't be afraid of educating differently than the norm. Be afraid of your kids not playing during their childhood.

You don't know what the final result of the adventure of living and growing without school will be. It's like connecting the dots in a coloring book. At first, the picture looks quite strange and you have no idea what it will look like. But as you keep tracing every single dot, you finally reach the last one and the picture suddenly becomes beautiful. It all makes perfect sense why you connected every dot. It happened to me when my son became a novelist and my daughter an aerialist. With my youngest I'm still trying to figure out where the dots are leading us. Prepare yourself for the unexpected. It can be a beautiful adventure with a wonderful ending.

Say goodbye to school and live.

You are not a teacher (and other judgmental comments.

There will always be people who judge others, no matter what choices they make in their lives. Whether it's about jobs, relationships, or even choices regarding pets, some people will always have something negative to say. However, people with an open mind and a lot of knowledge are less likely to judge you. They understand that everyone has their own unique circumstances and experiences that shape their choices and actions, and they are more likely to be empathetic and understanding. Those who judge you are likely insecure about themselves or their own abilities, and they lack knowledge of how children learn.

Alternative methods of education have already been tested and have succeeded. You don't have to explain your choice over and over to other people. It is your choice how to raise your children. In fact, it is a human right to choose the type of education you want for your children, and it is a human right to choose the education you want for yourself.

Teachers are quitting their jobs, more centers offering self-directed education are opening, and the home educating movement is growing. Numerous parents have educated their children successfully without being teachers themselves. People are judgy because they are not ready for growth and are unwilling to expand their mindset. They confuse a good education with molding children into a standard model, following the standards of what a model child should be. They don't know a good education is actually nurturing children's unique natural development and special qualities. You do not need to be a teacher to educate your children.

Although educating freely is not a novel idea, its popularity has grown significantly in recent years because of its adaptable and individualized approach to education. Unschooling enables children to discover the world and acquire knowledge through diverse avenues instead of depending solely on conventional schooling methods.

It is a pedagogical philosophy that promotes parental support as their children take the lead in their own learning journey as parents encourage them to investigate and discover their surroundings instead of adhering to a fixed curriculum. This approach fosters imaginative exploration, uncovering, and active participation in the environment. It is a fantastic way to educate. Don't let others' judging stop you.

My family and friends don't understand, don't agree, and criticize me.

It's such a shame when your loved ones don't respect your decision and criticize your choice every time they see you. In my opinion, a good friend doesn't criticize you, but supports you. Family is a different story. It's important to stop their accusations and try not to argue. It has been shown in books, doctoral theses, articles, and documentaries that alternative educational methods are successful, so you don't have to justify your choice continually. Do we ask families who send their children to school to explain why they do it?

Here are some statements you can use:

- "School may be a good option for some families, but it doesn't work for mine."
- "I prefer to educate without school, and it is a valid option and a human right." (Article 26 point 3 of the Universal Declaration of Human Rights of the United Nations states: "Parents have a prior right to choose the kind of education that shall be given to their children.")
- "There are many books written by doctors that talk about educating without school, a method that does not affect the intelligence or sociability of children."
- "There are many teachers and university professors who educate their children without school."
- "I don't want to argue about this with someone who hasn't studied education."

- "When you have researched and analyzed self-directed education, we can talk about it."
- "They are my children, not yours."
- "Everyone can educate their children as they see fit."
- "Don't worry, I know what I'm doing. There's a lot of research behind this topic, and many people have done it."
- "I respect your decision to send your children to school, please respect mine."
- If they ask you when you're going to send your children to school, the appropriate response is: "When they want to go." But if you feel sassy you can even answer, "When are you going to take yours out of school?"

My mother/mother-in-law is a former teacher. She's very vocal and opinionated and doesn't like the idea.

Engaging in conversations about alternative education methods with someone who has a background in teaching can be challenging. It's understandable that your mother or mother-in-law may have strong opinions and concerns based on her experience. Instead of trying to convince her all at once, consider having open and respectful discussions about your choice gradually.

Share the benefits and success stories of self-directed education with her, providing examples of families who have found it to be a positive approach. You can mention professionals in the field, such as psychologists and education experts, who have chosen to educate their own children without traditional schooling. Gina Riley, Kerry McDonald, Julie Bogart, Peter Gray, Naomi Fisher, and many others are among those who advocate for self-directed learning.

Encourage your mother or mother-in-law to explore relevant books, articles, and resources written by these professionals, as well as videos and testimonials from homeschooling and unschooling families. Let her know that there is a wealth of information available on this topic that she can delve into to gain a broader understanding.

Be patient and understanding, as her perspective may be deeply ingrained. Give her the opportunity to process the information and ask questions. Remember, changing one's mindset takes time, and it's ultimately her choice whether to delve into the subject further.

Remember that as the parent, you are the one responsible for making decisions about your children's education. While it can be challenging dealing with a strong-willed and opinionated family member, it's essential to assert your role as the decision-maker. Respectfully remind your mother or mother-in-law that you value her input, but you are the one who knows what is best for your child and family. Set clear boundaries and communicate your expectations regarding discussions about education. It's important to maintain your confidence and stand firm in your choices, even if it means respectfully disagreeing with your parents or in-laws. Remember, your children's well-being and educational journey are your top priorities.

I live in a country where educating at home is illegal.

Many people mistakenly assume that homeschooling is illegal in their country simply because it is not commonly known or not officially regulated. In reality, in many countries, while education is mandatory, there are no specific laws either legalizing or outlawing homeschooling, and families are able to homeschool without facing legal issues.

Unfortunately, some countries do absolutely prohibit it. There are articles that talk about German and Swedish families leaving their countries and moving to Ireland or the U.S.A., where home education is legal. I have a friend who left the Netherlands to educate her children freely. Together, she and her husband had to move countries twice to provide their two children with the opportunity of self-directed learning. They are currently based in Boston.

It's difficult to leave your country, but your children are worth it. Here is the story of my friend, Sophia.

I usually say our family are educational refugees. We have had to move countries to be able to homeschool and we are about to move across the Atlantic to be able to continue unschooling. We are seeking refuge from Europe's bulging institutional control over learning and development as we want our children to continue self-directing their learning process.

My elder son, Simon, has always been a self-directed learner, while I have assumed the role of a facilitator. We have never restricted the time he spent devouring educational apps and YouTube videos and often ran out of paper while he tried to recreate everything he had read or watched. The whole pavement around our apartment block in downtown Amsterdam was covered in Japanese Katakana, Greek letters, the Beaufort scale charts, units of measurement, and—most commonly—geometric shapes and formulas.

At the same time, Simon didn't seem to have much interest in playing with other children and was very asynchronous in his development of practical skills, which alarmed a few state-sponsored experts. For a while, we tried to play the "gifted" card to get him to spend part of his days in his school's mixed-age small gifted class. The gifted class teacher didn't particularly enjoy having him and frequently "forgot" to pick him up from his regular overcrowded kindergarten class.

In fact, most teachers didn't know what to do with Simon, who moved about a lot and didn't like following instructions. In his second year of school, when he was five, everyone in the gifted class was making Christmas cards, but Simon's was the only one the teacher didn't hang up to decorate the wall, because it wasn't Christmas-themed, she said. Simon's card depicted the map of Caribbean countries and islands that he drew from memory (his main interest that Christmas).

In the semester that followed, Simon's principal allowed him to spend most of his time at home, only coming to school for a couple of hours a day. The school could only pay for so many hours a day for Simon to be accompanied by a supervising psychologist and the gifted class teacher wouldn't let Simon take part in her classes without the psychologist to supervise him. What a huge waste of money it was, if you ask me. And what a great relief to see Simon thrive at home, with all the unstructured time on his hands!

At this point you may wonder, why didn't we just pull Simon out of school, for he was clearly not school material?

In the Netherlands, parents don't have the right to pull a child out of school. If they do take their children out of school, they may be taken to court, like criminals. I know many families who have gone through the hell of being accused of parental negligence after the school filed a complaint against them with the much dreaded child protection services.

In their uncompromising war on divergent parenting, the Dutch child protection services remind me of the Spanish inquisition. Many investigative reports, articles and even books have tried to shed light on this dark side of the Dutch society, including devastatingly inhumane cases in which children who are in no urgent danger are nonetheless withdrawn from their families by a police squad without prior notice, cases that don't allow for truth finding, cases where court judges seem to blindly follow child protection services with whom they sometimes work in the same building.

Over forty thousand Dutch children are growing up separated from their parents. This often implies having to change several foster families, developing severe attachment disorders, PTSD, self-mutilation, and suicide ideation. Nearly two thousand kids are currently locked up in closed jail-like institutions, the best way the Dutch state has found to "protect" them. "The Netherlands is a champion in locking up children", Hélène van Beek writes in her book Children of the State. *Children who did nothing wrong.*

As I am writing this, I have just signed the petition to abolish these locked facilities and "secure units". It would be wonderful if they became history. However, in my view, the locked facilities are but a symptom of a much deeper problem in the Dutch society: the state simply has too much power over family life and the legal system somehow tolerates that. The lack of trust in divergence is at par with a fetish for efficacy, risk aversion, and record keeping, make it a stressful place to live in if you want to do things differently.

Aged six, Simon became legally obliged to attend school full-time, but no small school wanted him. When we asked Simon's gifted class teacher to take him, her answer was, "Over my dead body!" Another alternative school Simon tried out for three days said he was too much work. Eventually, we found one more gifted school out of town that agreed to accept Simon on a trial period.

That year was the only time in Simon's life that I saw him start to wither. He just didn't have the fuel to light up any more. After the long bus ride back from school, he crashed on the sofa and just sat there, staring at the TV. The pavement around our block remained free of new writings more often than not.

Of course, there are plenty of cases when the Dutch school system would simply spit out the unchewable chunk and the child does end up staying at home after all, getting the honorable label of "unteachable" or "home sitter" and thus exempt of the "learning duty" (school attendance). However, we were told that our family couldn't count on that, because Simon "wasn't traumatized enough."

Luckily, we had done a lot of research and met many other families online who had been in a similar pickle. Simon's dear dad, my calm-as-a-rock husband, Steven, said he was okay with spending five hours every day commuting to his Dutch office. We decided to move to Belgium.

This was the best decision of my life, next to marrying Steven.

Once we moved to Belgium, it took no longer than three days to officially register Simon and his little sister Neva as homeschoolers. In a way it felt like entering another dimension: you cross the border and instantly you have your basic human right back to choose the way you learn.

The move was very hard on me. After all, I had already emigrated once, from Russia. Amsterdam had become an indispensable part of my identity as the Russian radio correspondent from the Netherlands. It *was hard to give up the network I had built up, to give up working all together. Yet, what were all those things worth if they came at the cost of my child withering in front of my eyes?*

Belgium used to enjoy total homeschooling freedom until home inspections and compulsory exams were introduced a little less than a decade ago. A stifling wave of increased government control over learning has sadly engulfed many European countries, whose governments seem to believe that fewer educational choices will lead toward better assimilation of newcomers. That said, the Flemish (Dutch) speaking part of the country continues to leave its homeschoolers in relative peace until around age twelve. Submitting your annual educational plan is all you have to do and the home inspections, no matter how unfair and intrusive they may feel, only take place once every two to three years.

We have relished our six years in Belgium. We started out feeling small, tired and shivery, scared to be denied, but the gorgeous city of Antwerp embraced us and let us be. As opposed to the friendly but nosy and judgmental Amsterdam, Antwerp didn't really care. And that was exactly what we needed in order to heal and rediscover ourselves. We have reemerged on the other end of the Belgian leg of our journey as a family no longer in need of validation of our children's giftedness, no longer anxious about their quirks and asynchronicities, but humbled by how meaningful our children's choices have been for their personal fulfillment. Antwerp is where we have learned to let go and to trust.

Today, as Neva and Simon are entering their teens, their main passion is game development. They have just published their first big game and are learning the Unity engine together to eventually build a new game in 3D. Simon, who taught himself trigonometry, logs, and derivatives before the age of nine, continues to explore math and computer science. Neva also enjoys coding, as well as composing game music. They are both actively collaborating with like-minded geeks across the globe.

Our home has the vibe of a creative studio as my children and I work on our projects alongside each other. Our unschooling lifestyle has empowered me to rekindle my love for drawing and technology, and I have completed several animation courses. With my two university degrees, I don't think I have ever learned as much as I have learned in the past years thanks to unschooling.

We want to continue living like this, to enjoy each other's finds and epiphanies, to joyfully sort out the unknown every day brings. We don't want to have to prep Neva and Simon for the compulsory exams in Brussels that they would have to take in thirteen subjects, following a curriculum that has very little relevance to their daily lives or hopes for the future. During the three-day battery of elementary school exams last summer, Simon was asked a question about letting out pants at the tailor's! Simon did well at those exams, even in French, but we don't want to repeat the experience for Neva. Besides, Neva doesn't want to learn French, so why force her?

Simon also passed one of the middle school exams (in math) with ease when he was nine but failed his oral English. "You speak like a native speaker, but we can't give you a passing grade because you don't want to answer the questions," the examiner told him as he sat there, crying in my lap. Their questions lacked logic, he told me later that night, in English. "I guess it was one of those false negatives," he added as he fell asleep.

We don't want Simon and Neva to be led by external motivations and to measure their self-worth by their test results. Most of all, we don't want them to get distracted on their beautiful journey of self-discovery.

In a few months, we will be moving to the U.S. Even though, similar to the European school system, the U.S. conventional school system suffers from some grave ailments that will eventually drive it extinct (little autonomy for both students and teachers, the same coercive ritual of graded promotions), you do have the freedom to step in and out of that system as you please. In America, unschooling is not a taboo. A plethora of opportunities exist for those who don't want to do school but do want to get credentials or academic degrees later in life. I want the kids to taste the air of unparalleled entrepreneurial thinking, scientific rigor, and personal responsibility that America still has to offer.

I don't know what this new chapter will bring. To quote Richard Feynman, "I don't feel frightened by not knowing things, by being lost in a mysterious universe without any purpose, which is the way it really is, as far as I can tell. Possibly. It doesn't frighten me."

Sophia Kornienko is a radio journalist and artist who uses the medium of animation to tell real stories. Check out Sophia at unschoolingfuture.net.

It's not that I feel that school is a good idea gone wrong, but a wrong idea from the word go. It's a nutty notion that we can have a place where nothing but learning happens, cut off from the rest of life.

—John Holt

NUDGES AND WINKS

IT'S TIME FOR ME TO LET YOU GO SO YOU CAN
move on to your next book. Before you go, here are a few
reminders:

- To give your children a successful education,
  believe it or not, you do not need much. All
  you need is to be observant, resourceful, and
  accepting. Observe your children. What are
  their likes, dislikes, and interests? What makes
  them happy? How do they learn? What makes
  them angry?
- Find the resources your kids will need according to your observations. Provide everything
  you can, give, offer, and share information, but
  do not force.
- Think, talk, and discuss things that matter
  to your children. Solve problems, learn from
  mistakes, and spend time connecting with
  others and engaging in the community. Your
  kids will learn. Their learning will be meaningful and lasting, because everything you are

doing relates to their lives, and they are making connections.

- Accept who your children are, what they like, and what interests them. Don't act like a teacher. Your role is to connect with your kids, note their interests, and provide opportunities for your children to pursue those interests.

- Live as if school doesn't exist (don't copy the school). Children are hard-wired to learn. When they are interested in something, learning takes place. You don't have to push, persuade, or force children to learn. They already want to. Humans are naturally productive, energetic, and curious to learn, given the freedom and space to be so. Don't turn everything into a lesson.

- Learning is a side effect of playing, pursuing interests, and developing passions. Don't place learning in the schoolroom and playing in the playroom. Don't divide time by "learning time" and "playtime" or "screen time." Learning is everywhere, all the time.

- Inspire your children instead of restricting them. Give your children opportunities to thrive. Try to say *yes* to as many requests as possible.

- Relax. Teaching and learning moments occur naturally, and they are precious. Whenever you think, "I should be doing more," go back to deschooling and detoxing your mind from schoolish thinking. Focusing on what each kid needs is doing more. Let your children pursue whatever engages them.

- Children are the guides of their education process. Be generous by trusting them to find their own educational rhythm, and let your children's potential reveal itself. Look at who your children are, and help them be amazing.

Go give your kids a successful education. Go help your kid be a student of life.

I'll be here if you need me.

Find me online at:
- tiktok.com/@unschoolingstory18
- instagram.com/unschoolingstory18
- twitter.com/Unschooling1
- martaobiolsllistar.com

You don't have to have school buildings in order to have schools and you don't have to have schools in order to have education.

—John Holt

STORIES TO HELP YOU DESCHOOL YOUR MINDSET

MANY BRILLIANT INDIVIDUALS THROUGHOUT history have achieved great success with little traditional education and lots of self-teaching fueled by their interests and passions. Here are a few stories of people who were driven by their curiosity and desire to learn. Each story shows you that the best learning takes place when the learner takes charge.

I hope these stories help you deschool your mindset.

Erik Demaine

Erik Demaine, named one of the most brilliant scientists in America, holds a master's degree in mathematics and a PhD. He was educated outside of the traditional school system, instead traveling with his family and pursuing his interests freely, which ultimately led him to computer science and mathematics. Demaine's interest in video games sparked his curiosity in computer programming, which in turn led to his passion for mathematics. Remarkably, he began university courses at the age of twelve and earned his bachelor's degree at the age of fourteen from Dalhousie University. He then went on to earn his master's degree at sixteen and his PhD at twenty from the University of Waterloo. Shortly after, he accepted a position as an assistant professor, making him the youngest person ever to teach at MIT.

Jacob Barnett

Jacob Barnett was diagnosed with moderate to severe autism at a young age and was not expected to read or tie his shoes, let alone live a normal life. Due to his Asperger's syndrome, he attended public school up to the third grade in special education classes, but he wasn't being taught and showed no interest in learning. This concerned his mother, who noticed that he was different in school than at home, where he displayed an interest in puzzles and maps.

As a result, his mother withdrew him from school and allowed Jacob to explore the things he loved—math and science. By the age of eight, he was sitting in on college physics courses, observing. Jacob eventually taught himself high school math in the form of algebra, geometry, and calculus in just two short weeks. He was a full-time college student by the time he was eleven years old.

At the age of fifteen, Jacob submitted his master's thesis and later obtained a PhD in quantum physics. He is now considered one of the world's most promising physicists.

Thomas Edison

Thomas Edison, one of the most famous inventors in history, is known for his contributions to the development of the electric light bulb, phonograph, and motion picture camera. However, few people know that Edison's mother played a significant role in his education by taking him out of school at a young age.

As a child, Edison had difficulty in school and was seen as a poor student. His mother, Nancy Edison, did not believe that the traditional school system was the best fit for her son's learning style. She noticed that he was curious and eager to learn, but he was not motivated by the rote memorization and rigid structure of the classroom.

Nancy decided to take matters into her own hands and began educating her son at home. She encouraged him to explore his interests and pursue his passions, giving him the freedom to learn in his own way. Edison's mother taught him the basics of reading, writing, and math, but she also exposed him to science, technology, and mechanics, which would later influence his career as an inventor.

Edison's education outside of the traditional school system allowed him to think differently and approach problems creatively. He became a lifelong learner and developed a deep curiosity for the world around him. Without the constraints of formal education, Edison was free to explore and experiment, and his mother's unconventional approach to his education helped him become one of the most influential inventors of all time.

Edison's story is a powerful example of how alternative

education methods foster creativity and innovation. His mother's decision to take him out of school allowed him to develop his strengths and pursue his interests, ultimately leading to his groundbreaking inventions.

Agatha Christie

Agatha Christie, the famous British author, had a learning disability called dysgraphia that affected her ability to write coherently. As a result, she struggled with spelling and grammar throughout her life.

Despite her dysgraphia, Christie was able to learn and learned reading on her own. She was home educated and later in her late teens, she received a traditional education at a finishing school in Paris.

Christie's success as a writer is remarkable, given her learning disability. She wrote sixty-six detective novels and fourteen short story collections, which have sold over 2 billion copies worldwide. Her most famous works include *Murder on the Orient Express*, *And Then There Were None*, and *The Murder of Roger Ackroyd*.

Christie's unique writing style and intricate plotlines have made her a beloved author worldwide. She is known for her "whodunit" mysteries, which keep readers guessing until the end. Her success as a writer shows that a person's learning disabilities do not have to limit their potential.

Charles Dickens

Charles Dickens, one of the greatest writers in the English language, achieved his success with minimal formal education. Born in 1812 in Portsmouth, England, Dickens was the second of eight children. His family struggled financially, and at the age of twelve, he was forced to leave school and work in a factory to help support his family.

Despite his limited formal education, Dickens was a voracious reader who was largely self-taught. He spent many hours in the local library and immersed himself in the works of William Shakespeare, Oliver Goldsmith, and other literary greats.

At the age of fifteen, Dickens began working as a law clerk and then as a freelance reporter, jobs through which he developed his writing skills. His first published work, a collection of stories entitled *Sketches by Boz*, was released when he was just twenty-four years old. He then went on to write many beloved novels, including *Oliver Twist*, *Great Expectations*, and *A Tale of Two Cities*.

Dickens' writing is known for its vivid descriptions of characters and settings, as well as its social commentary and criticism of Victorian society. Despite his lack of formal education, he became one of the most successful and acclaimed writers of his time, and his legacy continues to this day. His example serves as a testament to the power of self-education and the importance of pursuing one's passions.

Mark Twain

Mark Twain, born Samuel Langhorne Clemens, was a renowned American writer who is widely celebrated for his humor and wit in his works. Twain was born in 1835 in Missouri, U.S.A., and his father died when Twain was only eleven years old. Due to his father's death, Twain had to leave school and start working as a printer's apprentice.

Despite not having a formal education, Twain was an avid reader and spent most of his time reading books from the library. He worked as a printer, journalist, and steamboat pilot before he discovered his talent for writing. Twain's first success as a writer came with his short story "The Celebrated Jumping Frog of Calaveras County," which was published in a newspaper in 1865.

In 1876, Twain published his most famous work, *The Adventures of Tom Sawyer*, which was based on his childhood experiences in Hannibal, Missouri. The book was an instant success and helped establish Twain as a leading American writer. He went on to write many other works, including *Adventures of Huckleberry Finn*, *The Prince and the Pauper*, and *A Connecticut Yankee in King Arthur's Court*.

Despite his lack of formal education, Twain's writing was admired for its wit, humor, and insight into American life. He was a master of satire and used his writing to comment on social issues such as racism and corruption. Twain's legacy as one of America's greatest writers continues to this day, and his works are still widely read and celebrated.

Alexander Graham Bell

Alexander Graham Bell, the inventor of the telephone, was born in Edinburgh, Scotland in 1847, and he was educated at home until the age of eleven. In school, he found the compulsory curriculum uninteresting and left school at the age of fifteen without graduating. Despite this, Bell continued his education and pursued his interests in speech and communication.

Bell's successful discovery of the telephone is widely known, but his work in the field of communication went beyond that. He also developed a device called the photophone, which transmitted sound on a beam of light. Bell's interest in communication extended to working with the deaf and hard of hearing, and he developed a method of teaching speech to deaf students, known as Visible Speech.

Despite his lack of formal education, Bell's interest in communication and his dedication to his work led him to become one of the most influential inventors in history.

Albert Einstein

Albert Einstein is a well-known scientist who revolutionized the field of physics with his theories and discoveries. However, it may come as a surprise to some that he struggled academically in his early years. His teachers often criticized him for being a slow learner and labeled him as "mentally handicapped."

Despite this discouragement, Einstein persisted and found success in his own unique way. He had a strong interest in science and spent much of his free time reading and experimenting. He was largely self-taught and did not attend college until later in life.

Einstein's work in physics changed the way we understand the universe, but it was his persistence and determination in the face of early setbacks that helped him achieve his success. His story is a testament to the fact that formal education is not the only path to success and that a strong work ethic and passion for learning can take you far.

Benjamin Franklin

Benjamin Franklin, one of the Founding Fathers of the United States, is widely known for his many accomplishments, including his work as an author, inventor, and statesman. However, what many people may not know is that Franklin had very little formal education.

Born in Boston in 1706, Franklin attended Boston Latin School for a few years but was forced to leave due to financial difficulties. Despite a lack of formal education, Franklin was an avid reader who was largely self-taught. He worked as an apprentice to his older brother, a printer, honing his skills in writing, printing, and publishing.

In 1729, Franklin purchased *The Pennsylvania Gazette* and turned it into one of the most successful newspapers in the colonies. He also began publishing his own writing, including his famous *Poor Richard's Almanack*, which contained witty sayings and practical advice.

Throughout his life, Franklin continued to pursue his interests in science and invention, and made significant contributions in these fields. He is credited with many inventions, including bifocal glasses and the lightning rod.

Andrew Carnegie

Andrew Carnegie was born in Scotland in 1835, and his family immigrated to the United States when he was a child. He grew up in poverty and had little formal education, leaving school at the age of thirteen to work full-time. However, Carnegie was determined to succeed and began working his way up in the railroad industry, eventually becoming a superintendent.

Carnegie's real success came when he turned his attention to the steel industry. He founded his own company, the Carnegie Steel Company, and utilized new technologies to increase efficiency and production. He also implemented innovative business practices, such as vertical integration and cost-cutting measures, that helped him dominate the steel industry.

Despite his lack of formal education, Carnegie was a voracious reader and self-taught intellectual. He believed in the power of education and philanthropy and donated millions of dollars to establish libraries, universities, and other institutions aimed at improving education and promoting social advancement.

By the time of his death in 1919, Carnegie had become one of the wealthiest individuals in American history, with a net worth equivalent to $372 billion in today's currency. His success and philanthropy serve as a testament to the power of determination, innovation, and lifelong learning.

The perfect education for your child doesn't exist. You have to create it.

—Marta Obiols Llistar

DID YOU FIND MY BOOK HELPFUL?

Your review can make a big difference! Please take a moment to share your thoughts and help other readers discover its value. Thank you for your support!

WANT TO DIVE DEEPER INTO

my journey of educating my three children? Discover my story in 18: An Unschooling Experience and explore the transformative power of unschooling. Join me as I share my insights, challenges, and triumphs in creating an alternative educational path for my family.

"A solid memoir about working outside the traditional educational system."—*Kirkus Reviews*

"Readers interested in radically student-focused homeschooling will find inspiration in this reflective memoir."—*BookLife by Publishers Weekly*

"For anyone considering keeping their child(ren) at

home for their education, this book is a must. Reading this book is like sitting down with the author and learning how she accomplished what seems to many to be an impossible task. Marta gently guides the reader through the minefields of homeschooling."—*Readers' Favorite*